Microwave Recipes

Microwave Recipes

Cooking times for 500w/600w/700w microwave ovens

MARY NORWAK
Edited by Daphne Metland

foulsham
LONDON • NEW YORK • TORONTO • SYDNEY

foulsham
Bennetts Close, Cippenham, Berkshire SL1 5AP

ISBN 0-572-01773-1

Printed in Great Britain by Cox & Wyman Ltd., Reading, Berkshire.

CONTENTS

Introduction 6
Using a Microwave Oven 8
Cooking Equipment 12
Cooking Fresh Food 15
Blanching Vegetables for Freezing 22
Cooking Frozen Vegetables 23
Cooking Convenience Foods 24
Defrosting 25
Reheating Frozen Food 31
Leftovers 32
Quicktips 32
Soups and Starters 33
Fish and Shellfish 50
Meat 64
Poultry 82
Pasta and Rice 96
Vegetable Dishes 101
Sauces 113
Puddings 124
Cakes and Bakes 139
Index 158

INTRODUCTION

It is only fair to say that it has taken me a long time to get used to the idea of microwave cooking. The cooking method was so different from anything that I thought of as 'cooking' that I frankly could not believe that a microwave oven could produce the sort of meal I wanted. How could a chicken be cooked in 25 minutes, or a cake in 7, and be pleasant to look upon or delicious to eat? Like so many owners, I initially treated my microwave cooker with some caution, using it to melt butter and chocolate, reheat a plated meal, or cook an emergency 'filler' like a baked potato or apple for a hungry child.

However, as a busy mother and writer, I began to feel that I was not taking full advantage of what the cooker could do for me. It is still not really a magic box, and there are a few things that it will not do, but the oven does have a number of important advantages. Not only does it save a great deal of time, but also fuel, since it can save up to 75 per cent of normal cooking time. The oven takes no time to 'warm up' and heat is not wasted in the kitchen, neither does it spread cooking smells all over the house. The microwave oven is clean to use, never acquiring that greasy patina which haunts the conventional cooker, and it also saves using saucepans which cuts down tremendously on washing up. Even the dishes used in the microwave oven are easier to wash as food is not baked-on and hard. A real bonus to the keen cook is that many foods, particularly fruit and vegetables, have a marvellous flavour since they cook for a short time with the minimum of liquid.

I have found a microwave oven particularly useful in conjunction with the freezer which is now so popular in many homes. Raw materials such as meat can be defrosted, and so can commercially-frozen cakes and puddings. Pre-cooked dishes, both home made and shop bought, may also be quickly reheated, and this helps to give much more variety to meals in busy households which might otherwise depend on expensive quickly-grilled meat in the evening. The microwave oven is safe and very easy to use, and there is little danger of contact-burning. It may be used by children or old people to prepare a meal with minimum supervision, and this means that they are more likely to choose a balanced meal than a skimped one or a fattening sweet snack.

When you start using a microwave oven, be sure to read the manufacturer's instruction book carefully. Start by cooking very simple things, even boiling water or melting butter, or reheating plated meals, so that you become completely familiar with the machine's controls. Then start using the recipes in this book, always following instructions exactly, particularly cooking times. Try to get used to cooking vegetables and fruit in the microwave oven, and use it for making gravy, custard and other sauces. Soon you will find that you use the oven a dozen times a day, on its own or in conjunction with the conventional cooker, and avoid those mounds of dirty saucepans.

In preparing this book, I have had particular help from Michelle Kershaw of Lakeland Plastics who has provided valuable information and cookware, for which I should like to thank her.

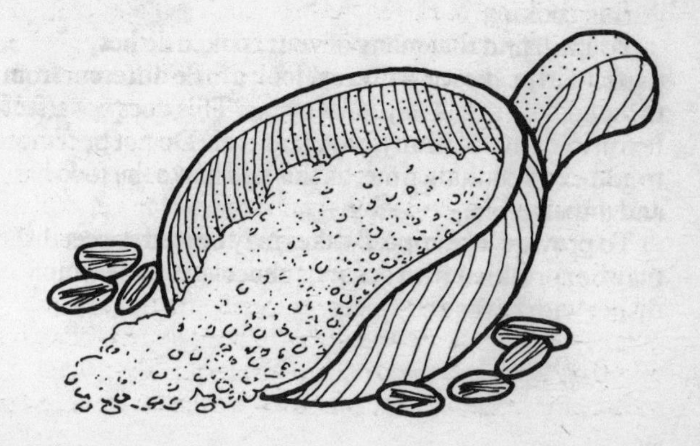

USING A MICROWAVE OVEN

The energy in a microwave oven is a type of high frequency radio wave. Microwaves are safe and do not damage cells, or alter the structure of food. Food is composed of water molecules and as microwaves enter the food they cause these molecules to vibrate at over 2000 million times a second, and the friction generates heat in the food. Microwaves penetrate from all sides to a depth of 1½–2 ins/3.8–5 cm, generating heat on the outside layers of the food which spreads by conduction to the centre. **This accounts for the 'standing time' often given in recipes, as food continues to cook for a few minutes after it has been taken from the oven. It is therefore very important not to overcook food such as cakes, which look undercooked when taken from the oven but which firm up after a few minutes' standing time**. Since there is no applied surface heat, however, food does not brown during short cooking times, although it will take place when a long cooking time is involved, such as in preparing poultry or a joint of meat. To counteract this, microwave recipes often suggest applying a rich baste, or sprinkling with spice or herbs, or spreading with icing, to disguise the paleness of food. Microwave browning spices are now available for savoury foods. A browning element, like a grill, is fitted into some expensive microwave cookers and may be used to pre-brown food or to brown it after or during cooking.

You will find that many of your cooked dishes, particularly cakes and breads, look a little different from those cooked in conventional ovens. This does not affect texture or flavour in any way, however. Do not be tempted to add extra cooking time, as this will make the food hard and unpalatable.

To provide 'eye appeal' cakes may be iced, sweet dishes may be sprinkled with sugar or chocolate, and savoury dishes with herbs and spices.

Types of microwave oven

Most microwave ovens are designed to sit on a work surface in the kitchen and can be plugged into a 13- or 15-amp socket. If you are likely to want to move it around it is best stored on a trolley, as most ovens are quite heavy. This way it can even be used in the garden for summer parties. A few microwave ovens can be built in above a conventional oven. There are also a few combination cookers in which the conventional and microwave cooking take place in the same oven, either separately or at the same time.

Controls and features

The most simple microwave oven has a timer and 'cooking' button, and works when the food is placed inside, the door shut, the timer set, and the button pressed. When the timer has moved to the 'off' position, or the door is opened, the microwave energy ceases. To restart cooking, the door must be closed and the 'cooking' button pressed again. The oven generally lights up when cooking begins, and the end of cooking may be signalled by a light, bell or buzzer.

Many ovens are supplied with a glass or plastic dish on the base which can be used to hold food, and which also prevents spillage on the oven floor. This plate should be kept clean by washing and drying often. A turntable is fitted in many ovens and is extremely useful as it ensures that food is turned evenly, and less manual turning and stirring of the food is needed.

Power control

The most basic models operate on constant full or high power. Variable control ovens enable power to be reduced to low or medium, which may be expressed in numbers, or labelled as 'simmer', 'reheat', 'roast', etc. A 'defrost' control button enables food to be thawed by exposing it to microwave energy for a short period, then allowing a 'standing' time, and repeating the processes as required without manual control. Consult your manufacturer's booklet to see what is the recommended cooking procedure for each labelled control. The 'defrost' control for instance may also be used for finishing slow-cooking stews; the 'simmering' control is also suitable for cooking delicate dishes such as eggs.

Preparation of food

Food will be heated or cooked faster if it is at room temperature. Chilled food will take longer to cook. Frozen foods may be defrosted first and then cooked, while some frozen foods such as vegetables may be cooked straight from the freezer. Most of the recipes in this book can be frozen, and the recommended freezing time is given after the freezing symbol (*). I have also included any special instructions to take into account before freezing the dish, together with thawing or reheating times.

Very dense food will take longer to cook than lighter dishes. If a ring mould is used for cooking a cake or pudding, this will help to transmit the microwaves to the centre. A dense piece of meat will take longer than minced or chopped meat. Food should be formed into the neatest shape possible so that microwaves are absorbed evenly, and for this reason a rolled joint of meat is preferable to an irregularly shaped joint. Poultry should have legs and wings tucked in closely to the body. Food which is in a thin single layer will heat better than food piled up.

Foods with a skin such as apples, potatoes and egg yolks, should be pierced before cooking to prevent exploding. If clingfilm is used to cover food, it should be pierced in two places to allow steam to escape.

Some recipes recommend that food should be stirred or rearranged during cooking to distribute heat in the food.

Timing

It is important to observe recommended cooking times carefully, and to resist the temptation to give a dish another minute or two, as one might with conventional cooking methods. This can result in dry and unpalatable food, or even food which is rock-hard. It is also very important to remember that the bulk of food makes a great deal of difference to cooking times, which it does not when using a conventional oven. A jacket potato for instance may cook in 6 minutes, but two potatoes will take nearly double the time, and three will take almost treble the time. Multiply the cooking time for such items according to the number of pieces involved, and then subtract a minute or two. If the food is undercooked, it may then be given another minute or so to complete cooking.

TIME ADJUSTMENT

The recipes in this book have been tested with a 600 watt output microwave oven and times are given accordingly. For a 500 watt oven increase timing by about 25 seconds for each minute. For a 700 watt oven decrease by about 25 seconds for each minute. For a variable control oven adjust to a suitable power level. But remember, all timings are approximate and it is better to undercook than overcook — dishes can always be returned to the microwave for a few more seconds.

TIMINGS CONVERSION TABLE

All timings are approximate

500 w	600 w	700 w	500 w	600 w	700 w
30s	20s	10s	15m 30s	11m	6m 25s
45s	30s	15s	17m	12m	7m
1m 25s	1m	35s	18m 25s	13m	7m 35s
2m 50s	2m	1m 15s	20m	14m	8m
4m 15s	3m	1m 45s	21m 15s	15m	8m 45s
5m 40s	4m	2m 20s	22m 40s	16m	9m 20s
7m	5m	3m	25m 30s	18m	10m 30s
8m 30s	6m	3m 30s	28m 30s	20m	11m 40s
10m	7m	3m 30s	32m 35s	22m	13m
11m 20s	8m	4m 40s	34m	24m	14m
12m 45s	9m	5m 15s	35m 25s	25m	14m 35s
14m	10m	6m			

COOKING EQUIPMENT

A very wide range of materials may be used in the microwave oven. One of the advantages is that food may often be cooked in its serving dish, which eliminates a great deal of washing-up. Although so many pieces of equipment may be used, however, it is very important to avoid metal, and also to choose the correctly shaped dish.

Metal

Metal dishes, trimmings or parts of dishes can cause arcing in the microwave oven which creates flashes of light and reflects the microwaves so that they will not penetrate the food. No metal dishes, baking trays, cast-iron casseroles or foil dishes should be used. Be particularly careful that there are no metal screws or handles on non-metal containers. A metallic decoration on a plate or mug can also cause the same problem, and so can metal twist-ties on freezer packs and cook-bags. Check with the manufacturer's instruction book though, as some allow small quantities of foil to be used.

Other materials

Ovenproof and ordinary glass, pottery and china may all be used. This means that a meal may be heated on a dinner plate, for instance. Pottery casseroles and baking dishes may be used. Plastic dishes which are suitable for a dishwasher are also suitable for the microwave oven, but food with a high fat or sugar content becomes very hot and may melt plastic dishes. Paper towels, cartons and pulp board are suitable for cooking and will absorb excess fat from the food, but wax-coated paper should not be used as the coating may melt. Freezer boil-in-bags and roasting bags are excellent for microwave cooking as they prevent food spattering and making a mess in the oven, but they should be closed with a twist of string or an elastic band

and not with a metal-based twist-tie. Allow plenty of space in the bag a some foods give off steam. Small bags will need to be punctured to release the air. Do not use melamine containers in the oven, as they absorb the heat and may char. Soft polythene containers may melt, as will yoghurt or cottage cheese containers.

Is the container suitable?

As a test to see if a container is suitable for the microwave oven, stand a glass of cold water in or next to the container being tested. Microwave for 1½ minutes. If the container feels cool and the water hot, then it is suitable for microwave use. If the container and water feel warm, the container is only suitable for short term heating as it is absorbing energy. If the container is warm and the water cool, then it is not suitable for microwave use.

Shapes

A round container gives the best results as an oval one will allow the food to cook more quickly at the narrow ends. Large shallow dishes are better than tall deep ones so that the heat spreads evenly through the food. Liquids, however, are better heated in a tall narrow container such as a jug, which should be large enough to allow for liquid boiling and rising. A straight-sided container is better than a curved one so that the microwaves penetrate more evenly, but the food must be stirred several times or it will overcook in the corners.

These are not suitable for use in conventional ovens, and also may become unstable if food with a high-fat or high-sugar content has been prepared as their boiling point is very high. These containers may be cleaned in the dishwasher, can be boiled and used in a pressure cooker. For freezing, they should be packed in a polythene bag. Many shapes are available. 2) Ovenboard ware is a range of polyester-coated paperboard which can be used in the freezer and microwave oven and which can also be used in the conventional oven up to a temperature of 400°F/200°C/Gas Mark 6. It is particularly useful as a substitute for foil cookware, and will not crack or shatter, or become soggy in use, as fat is absorbed and the special coating gives a non-stick base. The dishes remain rigid and are attractive enough to be placed on the table. 3) The newest development is in continuous usage microwave ovenware which has an attractive ceramic appearance. The range may be used in conventional ovens up to 400°F/200°C/Gas Mark 6, is non flammable, and will not melt or warp. It may be used in the freezer and taken straight to the microwave oven and may be cleaned in the dishwasher. A range of microwave accessories such as cooking racks and trays is available in polysulfone which can be used in conjunction with other cookware.

Browning dish

Food cooked in the microwave oven does not brown, but a browning dish may be used, which is ceramic with tin-oxide based coating applied to the surface of the base. This absorbs microwaves instead of transmitting them, and is ideal for browning small items such as chops, steaks and burgers. It is now possible to buy small tubs of microwave browning seasoning to sprinkle on meat and poultry prior to cooking.

COOKING FRESH FOOD

VEGETABLES

Vegetables may be cooked in a glass casserole dish or microwave dish, or in a roasting bag. They need to be prepared as for conventional cooking, and then have the addition of a little water or butter. Timings are for 600w ovens.

Vegetable	Quantity or weight	Cooking time
Artichoke (globe)	*1 medium*	*Remove stem and trim leaves. Add 4 tablespoons water. Cook 9 minutes.*
Artichoke (Jerusalem)	*1 lb./450 g.*	*Peel finely. Add 1 oz./ 25g. butter and 2 tablespoons water. Cook 11 minutes.*
Asparagus	*1 lb./450 g. medium spears*	*Add 2 tablespoons water. Cook 8 minutes.*
Broad beans	*1 lb./450 g. shelled*	*Add 2 tablespoons water. Cook 7 minutes.*
Broccoli	*1 lb./450 g. sprigs*	*Add 4 tablespoons water. Cook 9 minutes.*
Brussels sprouts	*8 oz./225 g.*	*Add 2 tablespoons water. Cook 8 minutes.*
Cabbage	*1 lb./450 g. shredded*	*Add 2 tablespoons water. Cook 10 minutes.*
Carrots	*8 oz./225 g. new whole or old sliced*	*Add 2 tablespoons water. Cook 10 minutes.*
Cauliflower	*8 oz/225 g. florets*	*Add 4 tablespoons water. Cook 5 minutes.*

Vegetable	Quantity or weight	Cooking time
Celery	*12 oz./350 g. sliced*	*Add 2 tablespoons water. Cook 9 minutes.*
Corn-on-the-cob	*2 medium, husked*	*Add ½ oz./15 g. butter and 2 tablespoons water. Cook 10 minutes.*
	1 cob	*Cook 8 minutes.*
	2 cobs	*Cook 11 minutes*
Courgettes	*1 lb/450 g. whole sliced*	*Add 1 oz./25 g. butter. Cook 4 minutes.*
French beans	*1 lb./450 g. whole*	*Add 3 tablespoons water. Cook 8 minutes.*
Leeks	*1 lb./450 g. sliced*	*Add 1 oz./25 g. butter. Cook 8 minutes.*
Mushrooms	*8 oz./225 g. unpeeled*	*Add 1 oz./25 g. butter. Cook 2 minutes.*
Onions	*1 lb./450 g. quartered*	*Cook 8 minutes.*
Parsnips	*1 lb./450 g. diced*	*Add 2 tablespoons water. Cook 10 minutes.*
Peas	*1 lb./450 g. shelled*	*Add 2 tablespoons water. Cook 8 minutes.*
Potatoes	*1 lb./450 g.new scraped*	*Add 4 tablespoons water. Cook 5 minutes.*
	1 lb./450 g. old cut in pieces	*Add 3 tablespoons water. Cook 6 minutes.*
(for baking)	*2 lb./900 g. scrubbed*	*Place on kitchen paper. Cook 20 minutes.*

Vegetable	Quantity or weight	Cooking time
Peppers	*8 oz./225 g. diced*	*Add ½ oz./15 g. butter. Cook 2 minutes.*
Runner beans	*1 lb./450 g. sliced*	*Add 3 tablespoons water. Cook 6 minutes.*
Ratatouille	*1 lb./450 g.*	*Add 1 oz./25 g. butter. Cook 9 minutes.*
	8 oz./225 g.	*Add ½ oz./15 g. butter. Cook 5 minutes.*
Spinach	*1 lb./450 g.*	*Cook 7 minutes.*
Spring greens	*1 lb./450 g.*	*Cook 8 minutes.*
Swedes and turnips	*1 lb/450 g diced*	*Add 2 tablespoons water. Cook 10 minutes.*

MEAT

Joints can be difficult to cook in the microwave oven because they are irregular in shape. A leg of lamb for instance is much thicker at one end, so the thinner end will overcook. It is therefore best, if possible, to bone and roll a joint and tie it into a uniform shape. Like poultry, meat may be cooked for preference in a large roasting bag which will prevent spattering and will help the meat to achieve brownness.

Meat	Cooking time
Pork, lamb, ham veal	*9 minutes per 1 lb./450 g.*
Beef: rare	*6 minutes per 1 lb./450 g.*
medium	*7 minutes per 1 lb./450 g.*
well done	*8 minutes per 1 lb./450 g.*

POULTRY

Whole birds and portions may be cooked quickly in the microwave oven, but a little care is needed in preparation. Be sure that birds or portions are completely defrosted, then rinsed in cold water and dried well. Poultry should not be cooked uncovered or it will dry out, and also splash grease in the oven. To achieve a brown skin, baste the bird before cooking with 1 oz./25 g./2 tablespoons melted butter into which 1 teaspoon soy sauce, 1 teaspoon Worcestershire sauce, and 1 teaspoon paprika have been stirred. Place in a large roasting bag and tie with string or an elastic band, leaving plenty of room round the bird in the bag. Stand the bag on a large plate. Cook for the given time and then drain off juices to use for gravy. Wrap the bird in foil and leave to stand for 20 minutes before carving.

N.B. Cooking time for game (rabbit or hare) is as for chicken.

Bird	Cooking time
Chicken and turkey	*8 minutes per 1 lb./450 g.*
Duck	*9 minutes per 1 lb./450 g.*

FISH

Fresh fish may be cooked quickly in the microwave oven. No liquid is needed, but a small knob of butter may be placed on each piece of fish. A little lemon juice may be added to white fish. Season after cooking.

Fish	Quantity or weight	Cooking time
White fish (cod, haddock, plaice)	*1 lb./450 g. prepared fillets, cutlets or steaks.*	*8 minutes.*
Oily fish (mackerel, trout, herring)	*1 lb./450 g. whole and gutted fish*	*6 minutes*
Smoked fish (cod, haddock)	*1 lb./450 g. prepared fillets, cutlets or steaks*	*7 minutes.*
Kipper fillets	*1 lb./450 g.*	*4 minutes.*

RICE AND PASTA

Rice and pasta are easy to cook in a large casserole dish with the addition of boiling water and butter or oil. The water may be boiled first in the microwave oven. A very quick meal may be prepared if a frozen or canned sauce is cooked in the microwave oven while the rice or pasta is standing after cooking, and no messy saucepans need to be used.

Food	Quantity	Cooking time
Rice (long grain)	*8 oz./225 g.*	*1 pint/600 ml. boiling water and 1 oz./25 g. butter. Cook 13 minutes . Let stand 15 minutes. Salt to taste.*
Macaroni (broken or elbow); pasta shapes; noodles	*8 oz./225 g.*	*1 pint/600 ml boiling water and 1 teaspoon oil. Cook 10-15 minutes. Cover and let stand 15 minutes. Drain off water. Season to taste.*
Spaghetti	*8 oz./225 g.*	*Break in half. 1 pint/600 ml. boiling water and 1 teaspoon oil. Cook 10-15 minutes. Cover and let stand 15 minutes. Drain off water. Season to taste.*

FRUIT

Fruit cooks well in the microwave oven and is full of flavour. Liquid is not needed for most fruit, but white or brown sugar may be sprinkled on before cooking.

Flavourings such as liqueurs or spices may be stirred in when the fruit has cooked. Cook fruit in a container covered with clingfilm with two small slits cut in the film.

Fruit	Quantity or weight	Cooking time
Apples	*1 lb./450 g.*	*Peel, core and cut in slices. Sprinkle with sugar. Cook 7 minutes.*
Apricots	*1 lb./450 g.*	*Cut in half and remove stones. Sprinkle with sugar. Cook 8 minutes.*
Gooseberries	*1 lb./450 g.*	*Top and tail. Sprinkle with sugar. Cook 4 minutes.*
Peaches	*4 medium*	*Cut half and remove stones. Sprinkle with sugar. Cook 4 minutes.*
Pears	*6 medium*	*Peel, halve and core. Add 3 oz./75 g. sugar dissolved in 6 tablespoons hot water. Cook 8 minutes.*

Fruit	Quantity or weight	Cooking time
Plums and greengages	*1 lb./450 g.*	*Cut in half and remove stones. Sprinkle with sugar. Cook 4 minutes.*
Rhubarb	*1 lb./450 g.*	*Cut in 1 in./2.5 cm. lengths. Sprinkle with sugar. Cook 10 minutes.*

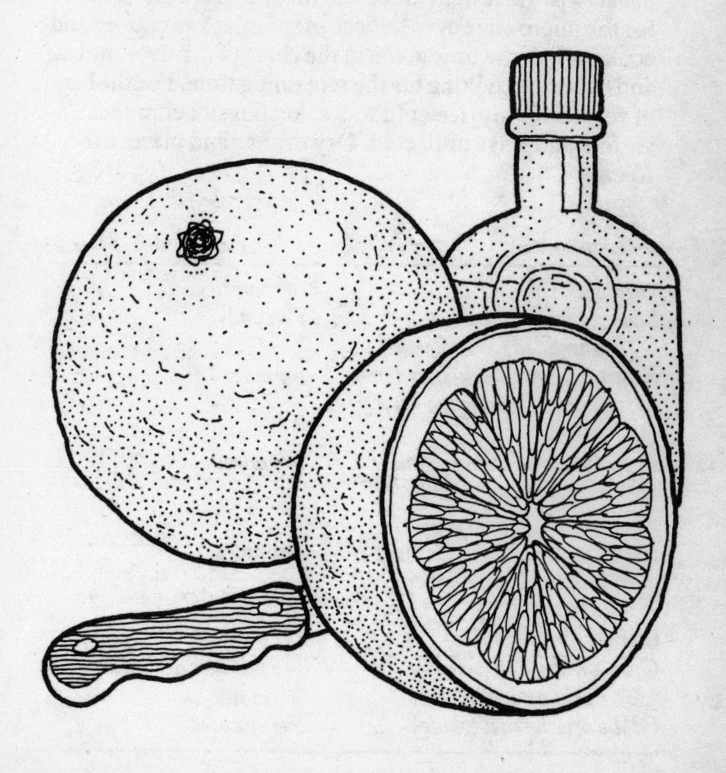

BLANCHING VEGETABLES FOR FREEZING

Vegetables must be blanched before freezing to retain their colour, flavour, texture and nutritive value. Vegetables may be prepared in the microwave which saves a lot of time and mess, and the easiest method is to blanch them ready-packed in bags. As with the traditional method of blanching, only 1 lb./450 g. vegetables should be prepared at a time.

Prepare the vegetables as for conventional methods of freezing. Put them into a heavy-duty freezer bag or boil-in-bag and tie loosely with a piece of thin string (the usual twist-tie fasteners contain metal and are not suitable for the microwave oven). Place in the microwave oven and cook for half the time given in the chart. Turn over the bag and continue cooking for the remaining time. Put the bag of vegetables into ice-cold water, keeping it below the surface and leave until cold. Dry the bag and place in the freezer.

Vegetable	Blanching time
Leeks (sliced); cabbage (shredded)	*45 seconds*
Runner beans (thick-sliced); spinach (young leaves); peas	*1 minute*
French beans (young whole); broad beans; root vegetables (diced)	*1½ minutes*
Asparagus; Brussels sprouts; broccoli; cauliflower (sprigs)	*2 minutes*
Carrots (small whole)	*2½ minutes*
Corn-on-the-cob (remove husks and silk)	*3–5 minutes according to size*
Globe artichokes (whole)	*3½ minutes*

COOKING FROZEN VEGETABLES

Always cook frozen vegetables without thawing so that they keep their colour, flavour and texture. Put salt or other seasonings at the bottom of the dish as it may dehydrate them if sprinkled on top (the seasoning will be distributed when vegetables are stirred). Put free-flowing vegetables in a shallow dish so that they form an even layer; large irregular vegetables such as broccoli should be arranged with the thickest parts facing outwards to the edge of the dish. If vegetables are in a block, separate half-way through cooking.

Very little liquid is needed to cook frozen vegetables, so do not increase the amount of water given below. Stir vegetables once or twice during cooking so that they cook evenly; they will also cook more evenly if covered with clingfilm which should have two small slits cut in it to release steam. When vegetables are cooked, they may be tossed with butter or cream and herbs, and if covered will keep warm for 10 minutes. Times are for 600w ovens.

Vegetable	Treatment	Cooking time
Broad beans, sliced beans,	*3 tablespoons water*	*9 minutes (1 lb./450 g.)*
Broccoli spears, Brussels sprouts, carrots, courgettes, peas, sweetcorn kernels	*1 tablespoon water*	*5 minutes (8 oz./225 g.)*
Asparagus, cauliflower sprigs	*3 tablespoons water*	*10 minutes (1 lb./450 g.)*
Whole or thick-cut beans	*1 tablespoon water*	*6 minutes (8 oz./225 g.)*

COOKING CONVENIENCE FOODS

Convenience foods are truly convenient when a microwave oven can be used for defrosting and/or cookin rapidly. Home-frozen raw materials and complete dishes and their commercial equivalents, can be quickly placed on the table and this considerably widens the choice of food for menus when cooking time is limited in a busy family. If foods are packed in foil, it is important to transfer to a microwave dish or non-metal serving dish; food packed in a polythene bag may, however, be defrosted and/or cooked in this container.

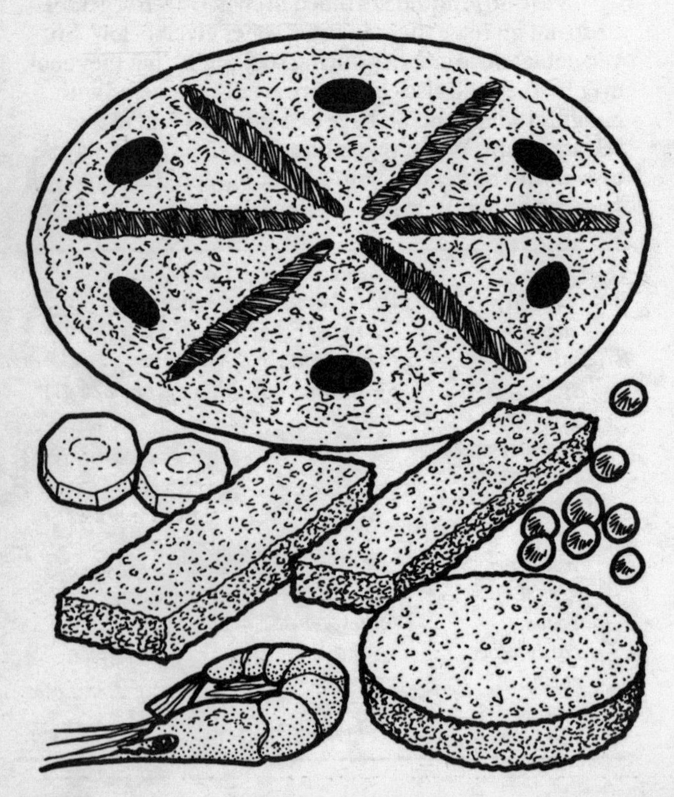

DEFROSTING

If your microwave oven has a 'defrost' setting, consult the manufacturer's instruction booklet for timing. If this is not available, use the 'cooking' setting, following this chart. Raw materials which have been defrosted (e.g. meat) may then be cooked by conventional methods such as grilling or roasting, or cooking may continue in the microwave oven. Some raw materials such as vegetables and fish need not be defrosted, but may be cooked from the frozen state in the microwave oven, and this of course applies to ready-frozen complete dishes. Instructions for these will be found on page 31 in the cooking chart.

Instructions for poultry (whole) and joints of meat will be found on page 28. Timings are for 600w ovens.

Food	Quantity or weight	Defrosting time
Bread	*Large loaf*	*Defrost 2 minutes. Let stand 6 minutes. Defrost 2 minutes*
	Single slice	*Defrost ¾–1¼ minutes depending on thickness*
Pastry (puff)	*14 oz./400 g.*	*Leave in wrapping. Defrost 2 minutes*
	8 oz./225 g.	*Defrost 1 minute*
Pastry (shortcrust)	*14 oz./400 g.*	*Defrost 2 minutes*
	8 oz./225 g.	*Defrost 1 minute*
Fish steaks	*3½ oz./90 g.*	*Cover with clingfilm. Defrost 3½ minutes. Let stand 5 minutes*
Fish fingers	*10*	*Remove from pack. Defrost 4 minutes. Let stand 2 minutes*
Fish cakes	*2*	*Remove from pack. Defrost 2½ minutes. Let stand 3 minutes*

Food	Quantity or weight	Defrosting time
White fish (e.g. cod, haddock, plaice)	*1 lb./450 g. prepared cutlets, fillets or steaks*	*Cover with clingfilm. Defrost 5 minutes*
Oily fish (e.g. herring, mackerel, trout)	*1 lb./450 g. whole gutted fish*	*Cover with clingfilm. Defrost 3 minutes*
Smoked fish (e.g. haddock, cod, kipper)	*1 lb./450 g. fillets*	*Cover with clingfilm. Defrost 3 minutes*
	1 lb./450 g. cutlets or steaks	*Cover with clingfilm. Defrost 4 minutes*
Chops (lamb and pork)	*2 medium (5 oz./125 g. each)*	*Defrost 2 minutes. Let stand 2 minutes*
Liver	*8 oz./225 g.*	*Heat 2 minutes. Let stand 5 minutes*
Minced beef	*8 oz./225 g.*	*Defrost 1½ minutes. Let stand 5 minutes. Defrost 1½ minutes. Let stand 5 minutes*
Chicken joints	*8 oz./225 g.*	*Defrost 3 minutes. Let stand 5 minutes*
Game pieces	*8oz./225 g.*	*Defrost 3 minutes. Let stand 5 minutes*
Sausages	*4 large*	*Defrost 1 minute. Separate. Defrost 1 minute. Let stand 2 minutes*
Roast beef in gravy	*4 oz./100 g.*	*Remove from foil pack. Defrost 2 minutes. Let stand 2 minutes*

Food	Quantity or weight	Defrosting time
Roast beef in gravy	*12 oz./350 g.*	*Remove from foil pack. Defrost 3 minutes. Let stand 3 minutes*
Whipped cream	*½ pint/300 ml./ 1¼ cups*	*Remove lid. Defrost 1 minute. Let stand 10 minutes*
Cheesecake	*Family size*	*Remove from foil pack. Defrost 1½ minutes. Let stand 15 minutes*
Mousse tub	*Individual size*	*Remove lid. Defrost 20 seconds*
Trifle tub	*Individual size*	*Remove lid. Defrost 35 seconds*
Dairy cream sponge	*1*	*Remove carton. Defrost 40 seconds. Let stand 5 minutes*
Cream doughnuts	*3*	*Remove carton. Defrost 35 seconds*
Jam doughnuts	*2*	*Remove carton. Defrost 1½ minutes*
Cream eclairs	*4*	*Remove carton. Defrost 45 seconds. Let stand 10 minutes*

POULTRY (WHOLE) AND JOINTS OF MEAT

Whole birds and joints of meat should be thawed on the 'defrost' setting, and time must be allowed for 'standing' so that heat penetrates the food without cooking it.

For chicken joints, chops and minced beef, see page 17.

Food	Quantity or weight	Defrosting time
Chicken	*2–3 lb./900 g.–1.5 kg.*	*Defrost 10 minutes. Let stand 20 minutes. Defrost 5 minutes. Let stand 10 minutes*
Game (whole)	*2–3 lb. 900 g.–1.5 kg.*	*Defrost 10 minutes Let stand 20 minutes. Defrost 5 minutes. Let stand 10 minutes*
Duck	*4½ lb./2 kg.*	*Defrost 10 minutes. Let stand 30 minutes. Defrost 6 minutes. Let stand 15 minutes*
Turkey	*13 lb./6 kg.*	*Defrost 20 minutes. Let stand 30 minutes. Defrost 10 minutes. Let stand 20 minutes*
Beef: joints on bone	*3 lb./1.5 kg.*	*Defrost 10 minutes. Let stand 20 minutes. Defrost 5 minutes. Let stand 20 minutes*
rolled joints	*3 lb./1.5 kg.*	*Defrost 10 minutes. Let stand 20 minutes. Defrost 5 minutes. Let stand 10 minutes*

Food		Quantity or weight	Defrosting time
	stewing meat	*2 lb./900 g.*	*Defrost 5 minutes. Let stand 10 minutes. Defrost 2½ minutes. Let stand 5 minutes*
	grilling meat	*2 lb./900 g.*	*Defrost 4 minutes. Let stand 5 minutes. Defrost 4 minutes. Let stand 10 minutes*
Veal:	*roasting joints*	*3 lb./1.5 kg.*	*Defrost 5 minutes. Let stand 10 minutes. Defrost 5 minutes. Let stand 10 minutes*
Lamb:	*joints on bone*	*5 lb./2.2 kg.*	*Defrost 10 minutes. Let stand 20 minutes. Defrost 5 minutes. Let stand 10 minutes.*
	chops	*2 medium (5 oz./125 g. each)*	*Defrost 2½ minutes. Let stand 5 minutes. Defrost 2½ minutes*
		4 medium (5 oz./125 g. each)	*Defrost 5 minutes. Let stand 10 minutes. Defrost 2½ minutes. Let stand 5 minutes*
Pork:	*leg roast*	*5 lb./2.2 kg.*	*Defrost 10 minutes. Let stand 30 minutes. Defrost 5 minutes. Let stand 20 minutes*
	loin roast	*3 lb./1.5 kg.*	*Defrost 10 minutes. Let stand 20 minutes. Defrost 5 minutes. Let stand 10 minutes*

Food	Quantity or weight	Defrosting time
chops	*2 medium (5 oz./125 g. each)*	*Defrost 2½ minutes. Let stand 5 minutes. Defrost 2½ minutes*
	4 medium (5 oz./125 g. each)	*Defrost 5 minutes. Let stand 10 minutes. Defrost 2½ minutes. Let stand 5 minutes*
sausagemeat	*1 lb./450 g.*	*Defrost 2½ minutes. Let stand 10 minutes. Defrost 2½ minutes*

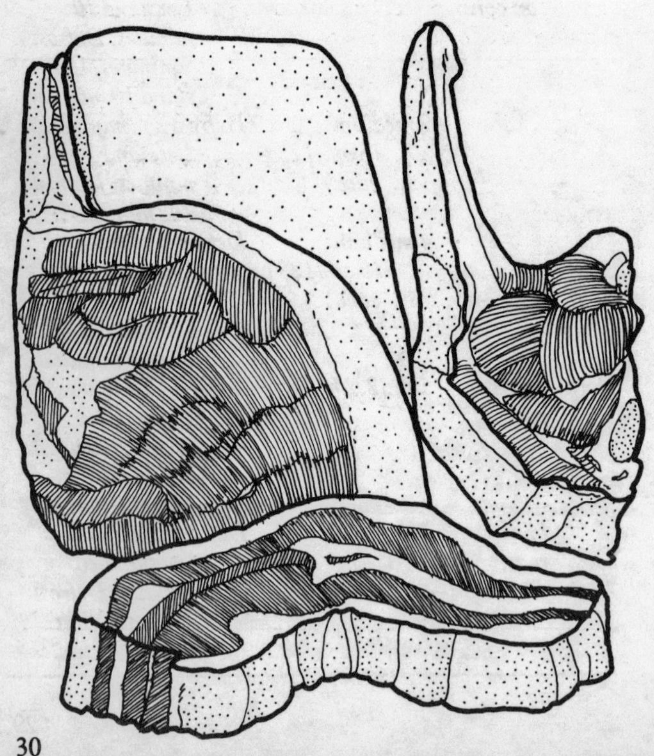

REHEATING FROZEN FOOD

If you have prepared cooked dishes for the freezer yourself, it is of course easy to see that they are packed in non-metallic dishes. Dishes are available in which food may be cooked in a microwave, frozen and then later reheated. Food may also of course be cooked in a conventional oven in everyday dishes or tins, and can then be transferred to microwave packaging for freezing and reheating. If a commercially prepared dish is packed in foil, the food must be transferred to a non-metal container before defrosting and/or reheating. It is important that the food should just fit into the new dish, as if the dish is too wide, the outside of the food will defrost and cover the base of the container, and will then start cooking while the main block of food is still being defrosted. Food which is packed in a boil-in-bag pouch may, however, be cooked in this packaging. Timings are for 600w ovens.

Food	Quantity or weight	Cooking time
Fish in sauce	*6 oz./150 g. portion*	*Pierce bag. Cook 5 minutes.*
Fish cakes	*4 × 2 oz./50 g. each*	*Shallow dish. Cook 4 minutes. Turn once.*
Meat casserole	*4 portions*	*Casserole dish. Cook 10 minutes. Break up twice during heating.*
Shepherd's pie	*4 portions*	*Casserole dish. Cook 10 minutes. Cover with foil and stand 5 minutes.*
Meat pies (cooked filling, uncooked pastry)	*4 × 2 oz./50 g. each*	*Square dish. Cook 6 minutes. Turn pies around two or three times.*
Spaghetti sauce	*4 portions*	*Casserole dish. Cook 12 minutes. Break up block.*
Soup	*2 pints/1.2 l.*	*Boil-in-bag placed in bowl. Cook 18 minutes.*

LEFTOVERS

Individual portions of cooked food may be reheated quickly, or a complete meal may be assembled on a plate. Single portions of such items as pies and cheesecakes should be covered with clingfilm on a plate and reheated for 30 seconds–1 minute. A complete meal on a plate of meat, gravy and vegetables should be covered and heated for 3 minutes.

QUICKTIPS

1. *Cocktail snacks* Make potato crisps and cocktail biscuits crisp again by heating 15 seconds in microwave. Let stand 15 seconds.
2. *Citrus fruit* Warm 10 seconds in microwave so that fruit is easy to squeeze and yields more juice.
3. *Coffee* Refrigerate left over coffee (made with coffee beans). For a fresh-tasting cup of coffee, pour into cup or mug and heat 1–1½ minutes in microwave.
4. *Leftover pies* Refrigerate leftover cold fruit pies. Put individual portion on plate and heat 1 minute in microwave.
5. *Biscuits* If they have softened, arrange a few in single layer on plate and microwave for 30 seconds.
6. *Dried herbs* Place a few sprigs of herbs or leaves between two pieces of kitchen paper. Microwave 2 minutes until dry and crumbly. Store in jars.
7. *Flaming puddings* To ignite Christmas pudding, etc., put brandy into a glass measure and heat 15 seconds in microwave. Pour over pudding and ignite.
8. *Blanched nuts* Heat ½ pint/300 ml./1¼ cups water in measuring jug for about 2 minutes until boiling. Add nuts and heat 45 seconds. Drain well, and slip off skins by rubbing with kitchen paper.
9. *Toasted nuts* Put blanched nuts in shallow dish with butter and heat 2–3 minutes until nuts are lightly browned, stirring occasionally.
10. *Softening dried fruit* Sprinkle with 1 teaspoon water. Cover and heat 20 seconds.

SOUPS AND STARTERS

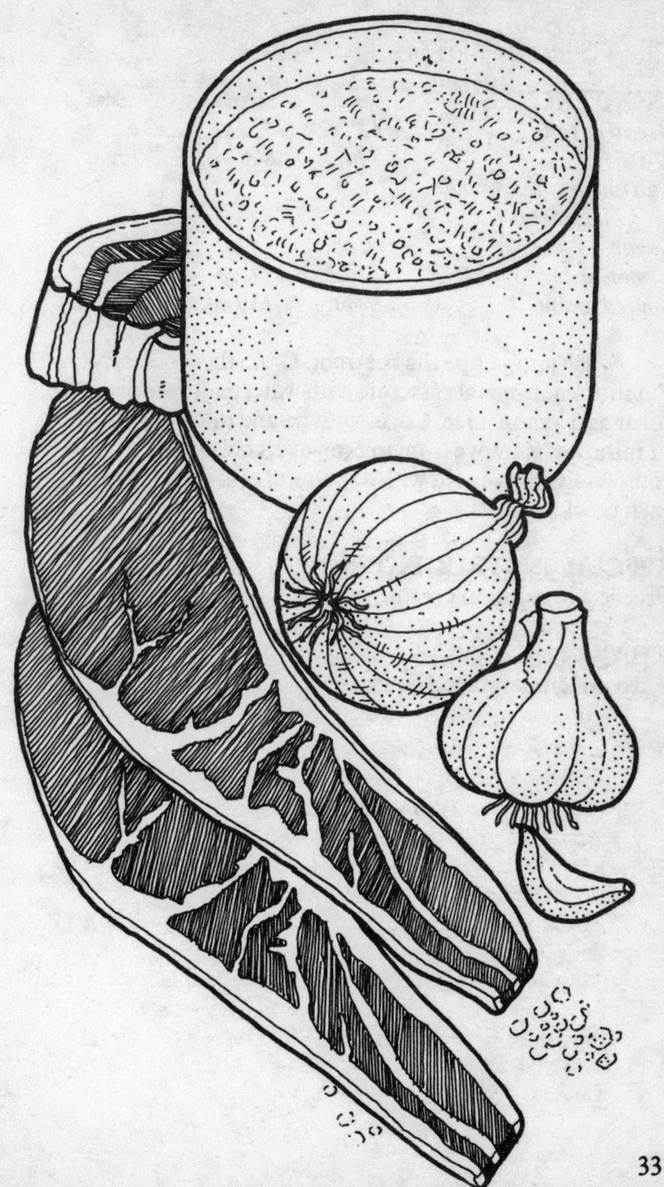

Borsch

✱ 2 months Serves 4

INGREDIENTS	Imperial	Metric	American
Beetroot (raw)	*12 oz.*	*350 g.*	*12 oz.*
Water	*1 pt.*	*600 ml.*	*2½ cups*
Salt and freshly ground black pepper			
Sugar	*½ oz.*	*15 g.*	*1 tbsp.*
Lemon juice	*2 tbsp.*	*2 tbsp.*	*2 tbsp.*
Soured cream	*¼ pt.*	*150 ml.*	*⅔ cup*

Wash and scrape the beetroot. Grate them coarsely. Put into a non-metal casserole with water, salt, pepper, sugar and lemon juice. Cover with lid and microwave for 12 minutes. Remove from microwave, cool and then chill completely. Serve cold with a spoonful of soured cream in each bowl.

SPECIAL INSTRUCTIONS
Freeze without sour cream.

THAW
At room temperature 3 hours

Carrot Soup

* 2 months Serves 4

INGREDIENTS	Imperial	Metric	American
Onion	*1*	*1*	*1*
Lean bacon	*2 oz.*	*25 g.*	*¼ cup*
Butter	*3 oz.*	*75 g.*	*6 tbsp.*
Salt and freshly ground black pepper			
Sugar to taste			
Carrots	*1 lb.*	*450 g.*	*1 lb.*
Chicken stock	*1 pt.*	*600 ml.*	*2½ cups*
Toasted bread	*1 slice*	*1 slice*	*1 slice*

Chop the onion and bacon finely. Put the butter into a bowl and heat in the microwave oven for 1 minute. Add the onion, bacon, salt, pepper and a pinch of sugar. Microwave for 5 minutes. Scrape or peel the carrots, and chop them finely. Add to the onion with hot chicken stock and microwave for 8 minutes. Put through a sieve or blend in a liquidiser. Reheat in the microwave for 2 minutes. Cut the toasted bread into small cubes, for croûtons. Serve the soup in bowls, sprinking a few croûtons on each portion.

SPECIAL INSTRUCTIONS
Freeze without croûtons.

REHEAT
18 minutes

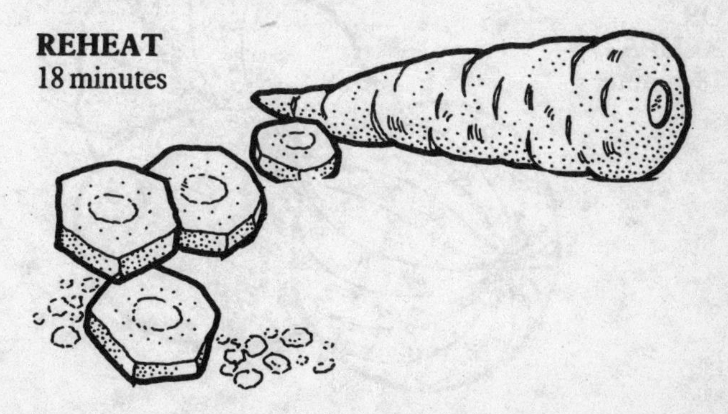

Garden Soup

✱ 2 months Serves 4

INGREDIENTS	Imperial	Metric	American
Potatoes	*8 oz.*	*225 g.*	*1½ cups*
Onion	*1*	*1*	*1*
Chicken stock	*½ pt.*	*300 ml.*	*1¼ cups*
Lettuce	*1*	*1*	*1*
Salt and freshly ground black pepper			
Ground mace			
Milk	*1 pt.*	*600 ml.*	*2½ cups*
Chopped mint	*1 tbsp.*	*1 tbsp.*	*1 tbsp.*

Peel and chop the potatoes and onion and put into a bowl with hot chicken stock. Cook in the microwave oven for 5 minutes. Shred the lettuce finely and add to the bowl with salt, pepper and a pinch of mace. Microwave for 1 minute. Put through a sieve or blend in a liquidiser. Put the milk into a jug and heat in the microwave oven for 3 minutes. Mix with the vegetable purée, and cook for 7 minutes. Serve hot or chilled, sprinkled with chopped mint.

THAW
At room temperature 3 hours
OR
REHEAT
18 minutes

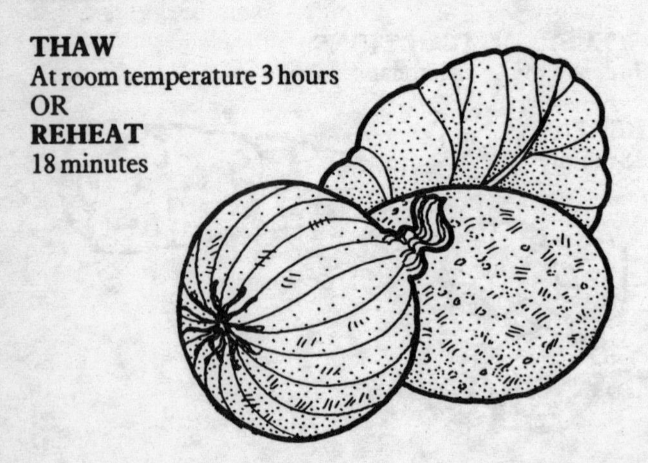

Green Pea Soup

* 2 months Serves 4

INGREDIENTS	Imperial	Metric	American
Butter	*1 oz.*	*25 g.*	*2 tbsp.*
Onion	*1 medium*	*1 medium*	*1 medium*
Frozen peas	*12 oz.*	*350 g.*	*12 oz.*
Salt and freshly ground black pepper			
Sugar	*1 tsp.*	*1 tsp.*	*1 tsp.*
Chicken stock	*1 pt.*	*600 ml.*	*2¼ cups*
Single cream	*¼ pt.*	*150 ml.*	*⅔ cup*
Chopped mint	*1 tbsp.*	*1 tbsp.*	*1 tbsp.*

Put the butter and finely chopped onion into a bowl and heat in the microwave oven for 3 minutes, stirring once. Add the peas, salt, pepper, sugar and hot stock. Heat in microwave 5 minutes. Put through a sieve or blend in a liquidiser. Reheat in microwave oven for 2 minutes. Stir in the cream and serve at once, with a little mint sprinkled on each portion.

SPECIAL INSTRUCTIONS
Freeze without cream and mint. Add just before serving.

REHEAT
18 minutes

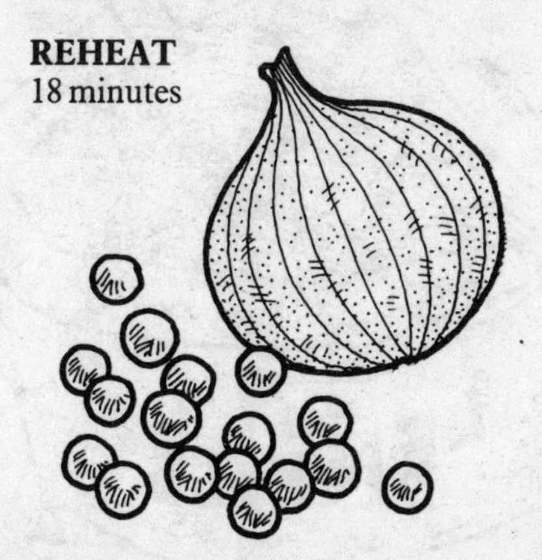

Lentil Soup

✻ 2 months Serves 4

INGREDIENTS	Imperial	Metric	American
Lentils	*4 oz.*	*100 g.*	*½ cup*
Bacon stock	*1½ pt.*	*900 ml.*	*3¾ cups*
Lean bacon rashers	*4*	*4*	*4*
Onion	*1 medium*	*1 medium*	*1 medium*
Celery sticks	*2*	*2*	*2*
Salt and freshly ground black pepper			
Chopped parsley	*1 tbsp.*	*1 tbsp.*	*1 tbsp.*

Soak the lentils in cold water to cover overnight, and then drain. Put into a bowl with hot stock, chopped bacon, onion and celery. Season well with salt and pepper. Cook in the microwave oven for 14 minutes, stirring twice during cooking. Put through a sieve or blend in a liquidiser until smooth. Reheat in the microwave for 2 minutes and stir in the parsley. Dried ham, or fried onion rings may be used as an alternative garnish.

SPECIAL INSTRUCTIONS
Freeze without parsley.

REHEAT
18 minutes

Italian Vegetable Soup

* 2 months   Serves 4

INGREDIENTS	Imperial	Metric	American
Oil	*1 tbsp.*	*1 tbsp.*	*1 tbsp.*
Carrot	*1*	*1*	*1*
Onion	*1*	*1*	*1*
Potato	*1*	*1*	*1*
Celery stick	*1*	*1*	*1*
Leek	*1*	*1*	*1*
Garlic clove	*1*	*1*	*1*
Stock	*1½ pt.*	*900 ml.*	*3¾ cups*
Spaghetti, broken	*1 oz.*	*25 g.*	*¼ cup*
Canned tomatoes	*8 oz.*	*225 g.*	*1 cup*
Grated Parmesan cheese	*2 tbsp.*	*2 tbsp.*	*2 tbsp.*
Chopped parsley	*1 tbsp.*	*1 tbsp.*	*1 tbsp.*

Slice the carrot. Peel and chop the onion and potato. Slice the celery and leek very thinly. Crush the garlic clove. Put the oil and vegetables in a bowl and cook in the microwave oven for 3 minutes. Stir well and add hot stock and spaghetti. Cook for 14 minutes, stirring twice during cooking. Add the tomatoes and their liquid and break them up with a fork. Continue cooking for 8 minutes, stirring once. Pour into bowls and sprinkle each with cheese and parsley.

SPECIAL INSTRUCTIONS
Freeze without cheese and parsley.

REHEAT
18 minutes

Onion Soup

* 2 months   Serves 4

INGREDIENTS	Imperial	Metric	American
Onions	*1 lb.*	*450 g.*	*1 lb.*
Butter	*1 oz.*	*25 g.*	*2 tbsp.*
Plain flour	*½ oz.*	*15 g.*	*1 tbsp.*
Beef stock	*1 pt.*	*600 ml.*	*2½ cups*
Salt and freshly ground black pepper			
Milk	*½ pt.*	*300 ml.*	*1¼ cups*
Chopped parsley	*1 tbsp.*	*1 tbsp.*	*1 tbsp.*

Chop the onions finely. Put the butter into a large bowl and microwave for 1 minute. Add the onions and continue cooking for 3 minutes. Stir in the flour, and then the hot stock, salt and pepper. Cook in the microwave oven for 10 minutes. Put through a sieve or blend in a liquidiser. Put the milk into a jug and heat in the microwave oven for 2 minutes. Stir into the onion mixture and reheat in the microwave for 2 minutes. Serve sprinkled with parsley.

SPECIAL INSTRUCTIONS
Freeze without parsley.

REHEAT
18 minutes

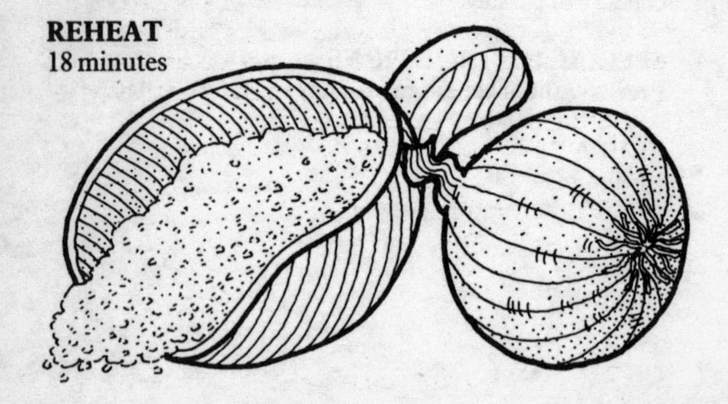

Spanish Summer Soup

* 2 months Serves 4

INGREDIENTS	Imperial	Metric	American
Tomato juice	*1 pt.*	*600 ml.*	*2½ cups*
Beef stock cube	*1*	*1*	*1*
Tomatoes	*2*	*2*	*2*
Green pepper	*½*	*½*	*½*
Onion	*1 small*	*1 small*	*1 small*
Wine vinegar	*3 tbsp.*	*45 ml.*	*3 tbsp.*
Olive oil	*1 tbsp.*	*15 ml.*	*1 tbsp.*
Garlic clove	*1*	*1*	*1*
Salt	*½ tsp.*	*½ tsp.*	*½ tsp.*
Worcestershire sauce	*1 tsp.*	*1 tsp.*	*1 tsp.*
Tabasco sauce	*Few drops*	*Few drops*	*Few drops*

GARNISH

Chopped tomato, cucumber, onion and green pepper.

Fried or toasted bread cut into cubes for croûtons.

Put the tomato juice into a non-metal casserole and heat in the microwave oven for 5 minutes. Add the crumbled beef stock cube. Skin the tomatoes and chop the flesh. Add to the tomato juice with the chopped green pepper and onion, vinegar and olive oil. Crush the garlic and add to the mixture with the salt and sauces. Heat for 2 minutes. Serve hot or cold accompanied by small bowls of chopped vegetables and croûtons.

THAW
At room temperature 3 hours
OR
REHEAT
18 minutes

Spinach Soup

* 2 months Serves 4

INGREDIENTS	Imperial	Metric	American
Butter	*1 oz.*	*25 g.*	*2 tbsp.*
Plain flour	*1 oz.*	*25 g.*	*1/4 cup*
Milk	*3/4 pt.*	*450 ml.*	*2 cups*
Chicken stock	*1/2 pt.*	*300 ml.*	*1 1/4 cups*
Ground nutmeg	*1/2 tsp.*	*1/2 tsp.*	*1/2 tsp.*
Grated onion	*1 tbsp.*	*1 tbsp.*	*1 tbsp.*
Salt and freshly ground black pepper			
Frozen chopped spinach	*8 oz.*	*225 g.*	*1 cup*
Single cream	*4 tbsp.*	*60 ml.*	*4 tbsp.*

Defrost the spinach at room temperature, or in the microwave oven. Heat the chicken stock. Put the butter in a large bowl and heat in the microwave for 1 minute. Stir in the flour and mix well. Stir in the milk, hot stock, nutmeg, onion, salt and pepper. Cook for 7 minutes, whisking 3 times so that lumps do not form. Stir in the spinach and continue cooking for 4 minutes. Put through a sieve, or blend in a liquidiser until smooth. Reheat in the microwave for 2 minutes. Stir in cream and serve.

SPECIAL INSTRUCTIONS
Freeze without cream. Stir in just before serving.

REHEAT
18 minutes

Tomato Soup

✻ 2 months Serves 4

INGREDIENTS	Imperial	Metric	American
Onion	*1*	*1*	*1*
Celery stick	*1*	*1*	*1*
Tomatoes	*1 lb.*	*450 g.*	*1 lb.*
Butter	*1 oz.*	*25 g.*	*2 tbsp.*
Plain flour	*1 oz.*	*25 g.*	*2 tbsp.*
Chicken stock	*1 pt.*	*600 ml.*	*2½ cups*
Tomato purée	*2 tbsp.*	*2 tbsp.*	*2 tbsp.*
Salt and freshly ground black pepper			
Basil	*1 tsp.*	*1 tsp.*	*1 tsp.*
Whipped cream	*¼ pt.*	*150 ml.*	*⅔ cup*
Chopped parsley	*1 tbsp.*	*1 tbsp.*	*1 tbsp.*

Chop the onion and celery finely. Skin the tomatoes, remove seeds, and chop the flesh. Put the butter into a bowl and heat in the microwave for 30 seconds. Add onion and celery and continue cooking for 5 minutes. Add the tomatoes and cook for 2 minutes. Stir in the flour and hot chicken stock with the tomato purée. Cook in the microwave oven for 5 minutes and then season well. Serve in bowls with a spoonful of cream and a sprinkling of parsley on each portion.

SPECIAL INSTRUCTIONS
Freeze without cream and parsley. Add just before serving.

REHEAT
18 minutes

Chicken Liver Pâté

* 2 months   Serves 4

INGREDIENTS	Imperial	Metric	American
Onion	*1 medium*	*1 medium*	*1 medium*
Garlic clove	*1*	*1*	*1*
Butter	*1 oz.*	*25 g.*	*2 tbsp.*
Oil	*1 tbsp.*	*15 ml.*	*1 tbsp.*
Chicken livers	*12 oz.*	*350 g.*	*12 oz.*
Salt and freshly ground pepper			
Ground mace			
Brandy	*1 tbsp.*	*1 tbsp.*	*1 tbsp.*

Chop the onion finely and crush the garlic. Put the onion, garlic, butter and oil into a bowl and cook in the microwave oven for 3 minutes, stirring once. Add the chicken livers and continue cooking for 4 minutes, stirring twice. Cool for 5 minutes and season with salt, pepper and a generous pinch of ground mace. Add the brandy and stir well. Put through a sieve or blend in a liquidiser. Press into a serving dish or individual dishes and smooth the top. Garnish with a thin slice of lemon or cucumber, or cover the top of the pâté with a little melted butter. Serve cold with toast.

SPECIAL INSTRUCTIONS
Freeze without garnish.

THAW
At room temperature 3 hours

Kipper Pâté

✱ 2 months Serves 4

INGREDIENTS	Imperial	Metric	American
Frozen kipper fillets	*6 oz.*	*150 g.*	*6 oz.*
Butter	*1 oz.*	*25 g.*	*1 oz.*
Lemon juice	*2 tsp.*	*10 ml.*	*2 tsp.*
Garlic clove	*1*	*1*	*1*
Brandy	*1 tbsp.*	*15 ml.*	*1 tbsp.*
Tabasco sauce	*Few drops*	*Few drops*	*Few drops*
Single cream	*2 tbsp.*	*30 ml.*	*2 tbsp.*
Lemon	*½*	*½*	*½*

Cut the corner of the boil-in-bag containing the kipper fillets, so that steam will escape. Put the bag on a plate and cook in the microwave oven for 5 minutes. Remove the fillets and take off any dark skin. Press through a sieve or put into a liquidiser. Add lemon juice, crushed garlic, brandy, Tabasco sauce and cream, and mix or blend until smooth. Press into a serving dish or individual dishes. Garnish with thin slices of lemon, or cover with a thin layer of melted butter. Chill and serve with hot toast.

SPECIAL INSTRUCTIONS
Freeze without garnish.

THAW
At room temperature 3 hours

Golden Grapefruit

Serves 4

INGREDIENTS	Imperial	Metric	American
Grapefruit	2	2	2
Medium sherry	*1 tbsp.*	*1 tbsp.*	*1 tbsp.*
Dark soft brown sugar	*4 tsp.*	*4 tsp.*	*4 tsp.*
Butter	*2 tsp.*	*2 tsp.*	*2 tsp.*

Cut the grapefruit in halves and remove pips. Cut carefully round segments with a sharp knife to loosen them. Sprinkle with sherry and sugar and leave to stand for 30 minutes. Cut the butter in small flakes and dot on top of each grapefruit half. Heat in the microwave oven for 3 minutes. The grapefruit may be garnished with a fresh mint leaf or glacé cherry.

SPECIAL INSTRUCTIONS
Do not freeze.

Country Pâté

✱ 2 months Serves 4

INGREDIENTS	Imperial	Metric	American
Pigs' liver	*8 oz.*	*225 g.*	*8 oz.*
Salt pork	*8 oz.*	*225 g.*	*8 oz.*
Onion	*1 small*	*1 small*	*1 small*
Garlic clove	*1*	*1*	*1*
Freshly ground black pepper			
Ground nutmeg			
Bay leaf	*1*	*1*	*1*
Streaky bacon rashers	*5*	*5*	*5*

Mince the liver, pork and onion finely. Put into a bowl and cook in the microwave oven for 5 minutes, stirring once during cooking. Crush the garlic and mix with the meats, and season well with pepper and nutmeg. Place the bay leaf on the base of a soufflé dish. Remove the rind from the bacon, and stretch out the rashers thinly with a flat-bladed knife. Arrange the bacon so that each rasher goes down one side of the dish, across the bottom and up the other side. Put in the meat mixture and fold surplus bacon over the top. Cover with a piece of clingfilm and cook in the microwave oven for 10 minutes. Leave to stand for 5 minutes. Remove the clingfilm and place a piece of greaseproof paper or foil on top of the pâté. Put a small plate on top and then heavy weights (cans of food will do if you have no scale weights). Cool and then keep in the refrigerator overnight. Turn out on to a serving plate and cut in wedges to serve with toast or salad.

THAW
At room temperature 4 hours

Smoked Haddock Pâté

* 2 months Serves 4

INGREDIENTS	Imperial	Metric	American
Frozen smoked haddock fillets	*6 oz.*	*150 g.*	*6 oz.*
Butter	*3 oz.*	*75 g.*	*6 tbsp.*
Plain flour	*1 oz.*	*25 g.*	*2 tbsp.*
Milk	*½ pt.*	*300 ml.*	*1¼ cups*
Single cream	*2 tbsp.*	*30 ml.*	*2 tbsp.*
Dry sherry	*1 tbsp.*	*15 ml.*	*1 tbsp.*
Salt and freshly ground black pepper			

Cut the corner of the boil-in-bag containing the haddock fillets, so that steam will escape. Put the bag on a plate and cook in the microwave oven for 5 minutes. Remove any skin from the fish and break the flesh into flakes. Put 1 oz./25 g./2 tablespoons butter in a bowl in the microwave oven and melt for 1 minute. Stir in the flour and then the milk and whisk well. Cook in the microwave oven for 4 minutes, whisking the sauce three times during cooking. Put the fish into a blender and add the sauce, remaining butter, cream, sherry and seasoning. Blend until smooth and creamy. Pour into a serving dish or individual dishes. Garnish with thin slices of cucumber or a few prawns. Chill before serving with hot toast and butter.

SPECIAL INSTRUCTIONS
Freeze without garnish.

THAW
At room temperature 3 hours

Mackerel Pots

* 1 month Serves 4

INGREDIENTS	Imperial	Metric	American
Smoked mackerel fillets	2	2	2
Butter	*½ oz.*	*15 g.*	*1 tbsp.*
Plain flour	*½ oz.*	*15 g.*	*1 tbsp.*
Milk	*½ pt.*	*300 ml.*	*1½ cups*
Cheddar cheese, finely grated	*1½ oz.*	*40 g.*	*¼ cup*
Salt and freshly ground black pepper			
Pinch of mustard powder			

Remove the skin from the mackerel fillets, and break the flesh into small pieces. Put the butter into a bowl and microwave for 30 seconds. Stir in the flour and the milk and microwave for 2 minutes, stirring twice during cooking. Remove from the oven and whisk well. Retain a little cheese for finishing the dish, and fold the rest into the sauce, with the salt, pepper and mustard. Fold in the pieces of fish. Put the mixture into 4 individual serving dishes, and sprinkle with reserved cheese. Microwave for 2 minutes. Serve hot with toast.

SPECIAL INSTRUCTIONS
Freeze without cheese topping. Sprinkle on cheese before reheating.

REHEAT
10 minutes

FISH AND SHELLFISH

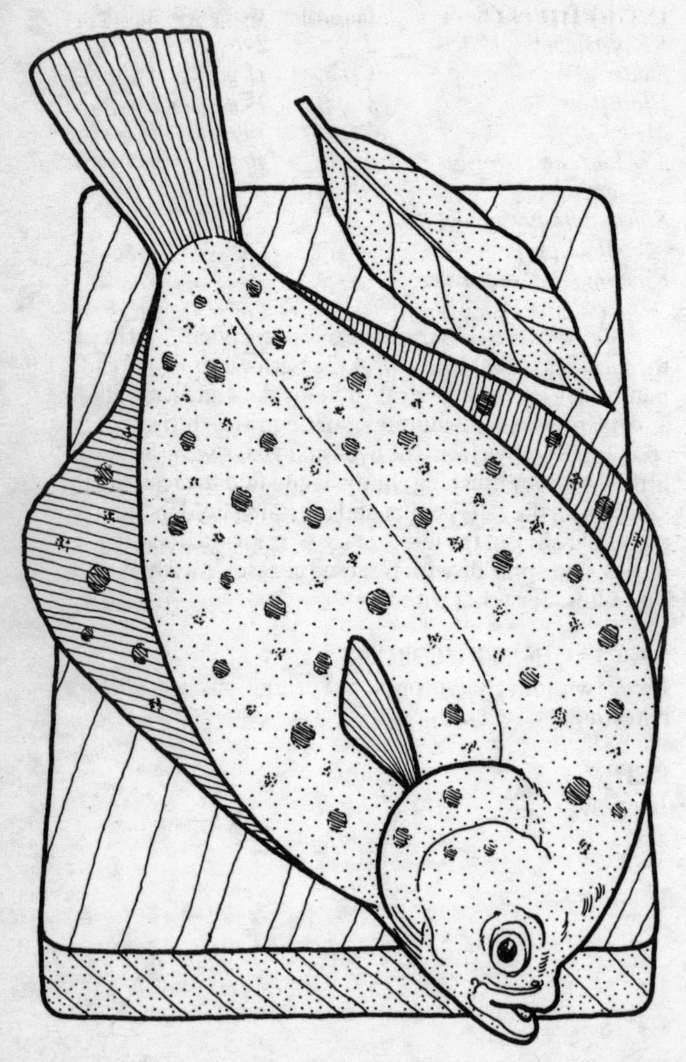

Southern Cod

* 1 month Serves 4

INGREDIENTS	Imperial	Metric	American
Cod fillets	*1 lb.*	*450 g.*	*1 lb.*
Oil	*1 tbsp.*	*15 ml.*	*1 tbsp.*
Onion	*1 medium*	*1 medium*	*1 medium*
Garlic clove	*1*	*1*	*1*
Tomatoes	*2*	*2*	*2*
Salt and pepper			
Sprig of basil			
Dry white wine	*¼ pt.*	*150 ml.*	*⅔ cup*
Black olives	*2 oz.*	*50 g.*	*½ cup*
Chopped fresh parsley	*1 tbsp.*	*1 tbsp.*	*1 tbsp.*

Remove skin from the cod and cut the flesh in 1 in./2.5 cm. cubes. Put into a casserole with the oil. Chop the onion finely and crush the garlic, and put into the casserole. Cover and cook in the microwave oven for 3 minutes, stirring twice. Skin the tomatoes and cut them in thick slices. Arrange on top of the fish and season with salt and pepper. Add the basil and wine. Cover and cook for 2 minutes. Stone the olives and add to the casserole. Microwave for 1 minute. Sprinkle with chopped parsley before serving.

SPECIAL INSTRUCTIONS
Freeze without olives or parsley. Stir in just before serving.

REHEAT
15 minutes

Cod in Cider Sauce

* 1 month Serves 4

INGREDIENTS	Imperial	Metric	American
Cod or haddock fillets	*1 lb.*	*450 g.*	*1 lb.*
Onion	*1 medium*	*1 medium*	*1 medium*
Button mushrooms	*4 oz.*	*100 g.*	*4 oz.*
Butter	*1½ oz.*	*40 g.*	*3 tbsp.*
Dry cider	*½ pt.*	*300 ml.*	*1¼ cups*
Salt and pepper			
Plain flour	*½ oz.*	*15 g.*	*1 tbsp.*
Double cream	*4 tbsp.*	*60 ml.*	*4 tbsp.*
Chopped fresh parsley	*1 tbsp.*	*1 tbsp.*	*1 tbsp.*

Skin the fish and place in a shallow dish. Chop the onion finely and slice the mushrooms thinly. Arrange on the fish. Cut 1 oz./25 g./2 tablespoons butter into thin flakes and place on the vegetables. Pour over the cider and season with salt and pepper. Cook in the microwave oven for 5 minutes. Lift the fish out of the dish and put on to a warm serving dish. Continue cooking the vegetables in cider for 5 minutes. Mix the remaining butter with the flour and stir into the liquid. Continue cooking for 1 minute, stirring once. Stir in the cream and parsley and pour over the fish.

SPECIAL INSTRUCTIONS
Put fish in freezer container. Prepare sauce without cream. Stir in cream and parsley after reheating.

REHEAT
15 minutes

Cod in Grapefruit Sauce

* 1 month Serves 4

INGREDIENTS	Imperial	Metric	American
Cod steaks	*4 × 6 oz.*	*4 × 150 g.*	*4 × 6 oz.*
Unsweetened grapefruit juice	*¼ pt.*	*150 ml.*	*⅔ cup*
Butter	*2 oz.*	*50 g.*	*4 tbsp.*
Salt and pepper			
Thyme (dried)	*¼ tsp.*	*¼ tsp.*	*¼tsp.*
Fresh white breadcrumbs	*1½ oz.*	*40 g.*	*¾ cup*
Grapefruit	*1*	*1*	*1*
Paprika			

Dip each cod steak in the grapefruit juice and arrange in a greased shallow dish so that they do not overlap. Cover with clingfilm and make two small holes in the film. Cook in microwave oven for 7 minutes. Drain off any surplus liquid and discard. Put the butter into a bowl and microwave for 30 seconds. Stir in salt, pepper, thyme, breadcrumbs and remaining grapefruit juice. Spread this mixture evenly over the fish. Peel the grapefruit and remove segments carefully so that there is no skin or pith attached. Arrange a few fruit sections on each piece of fish. Microwave for 2 minutes. Sprinkle with paprika before serving.

SPECIAL INSTRUCTIONS
Freeze without paprika. Sprinkle on paprika after reheating.

REHEAT
20 minutes

Baked Mackerel or Herring

* 1 month Serves 4

INGREDIENTS	Imperial	Metric	American
Mackerel or herring	*4*	*4*	*4*
Onion	*1 large*	*1 large*	*1 large*
Vinegar	*¼ pt.*	*150 ml.*	*⅔ cup*
Water	*¼ pt.*	*150 ml.*	*⅔ cup*
Salt and pepper			
Bay leaves	2	2	2
Lemon wedges to garnish			

Clean the mackerel or herring and remove the backbone. Slice the onion very thinly and place in a shallow dish. Mix the vinegar and water and season well. Pour over the onion slices and put the bay leaves on top. Put two mackerel or herring on top and cook in the microwave oven for 8 minutes, turning the fish two or three times during cooking. Lift the fish on to a serving dish. Put the last two fish into the liquid and microwave for 8 minutes. Put these fish on to the serving dish. Garnish with a few of the onion rings and some lemon wedges and serve cold with salad.

THAW
At room temperature 3 hours

Kedgeree

* 1 month Serves 4

INGREDIENTS	Imperial	Metric	American
Smoked haddock fillets	*1 lb.*	*450 g.*	*1 lb.*
Boiling water	*1 pt.*	*600 ml.*	*2½ cups*
Butter	*1 oz.*	*25 g.*	*2 tbsp.*
Onion	*1 medium*	*1 medium*	*1 medium*
Long grain rice	*6 oz.*	*150 g.*	*¾ cup*
Bay leaf	*1*	*1*	*1*
Salt and freshly ground pepper			
Garnish			
Hard-boiled eggs	*3*	*3*	*3*
Chopped fresh parsley	*1 tbsp.*	*1 tbsp.*	*1 tbsp.*
Butter	*2 oz.*	*50 g.*	*4 tbsp.*

Put the haddock into a shallow dish and cover with the boiling water. Cook in the microwave oven for 5 minutes. Reserve the cooking liquid. Take any skin from the fish, and flake the flesh. Put the butter into a casserole dish and heat in the microwave oven for 1 minute. Add the finely chopped onion and microwave for 2 minutes. Add the rice and bay leaf and pour on the cooking liquid. Cook for 15 minutes, stirring twice, until the liquid has been absorbed. Take out and discard the bay leaf. Stir in the fish, and season well. Chop the hard-boiled eggs and stir into the rice with the parsley and butter cut into small flakes. Microwave for 1 minute and serve at once.

SPECIAL INSTRUCTIONS
Freeze without garnish. Stir in after reheating.

REHEAT
20 minutes

Poached Salmon

* 1 month Serves 4

INGREDIENTS	Imperial	Metric	American
Salmon steaks	*4 × 6 oz.*	*4 × 150 g.*	*4 × 6 oz.*
Water	*¼ pt.*	*150 ml.*	*⅔ cup*
Lemon juice	*1 tbsp.*	*1 tbsp.*	*1 tbsp.*
Pinch of salt			
Thin slices of cucumber and lemon to to garnish			

Place the salmon steaks in a shallow dish. Pour over the water and lemon juice and add the salt. Cover with clingfilm and make two small holes in the film. Cook in the microwave oven 7 minutes. Take out of the oven and leave to stand in the liquid for 5 minutes. Lift on to serving dish, draining well, and serve hot or cold with Hollandaise sauce or mayonnaise. Garnish with lemon and cucumber slices.

THAW
At room temperature 3 hours

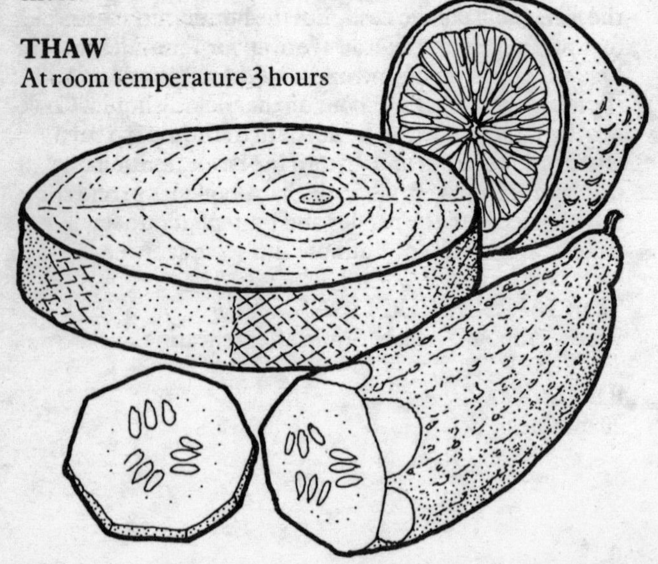

Trout in Wine Sauce

* 1 month Serves 4

INGREDIENTS	Imperial	Metric	American
Trout	*4 × 8 oz.*	*4 × 225 g.*	*4 × 8 oz.*
Salt and pepper			
Butter	*1 oz.*	*25 g.*	*2 tbsp.*
Chopped fresh parsley	*1 tbsp.*	*1 tbsp.*	*1 tbsp.*
Grated lemon rind	*1 tbsp.*	*1 tbsp.*	*1 tbsp.*
Dry white wine	*¼ pt.*	*150 ml.*	*⅔ cup*
Cornflour	*1 tsp.*	*1 tsp.*	*1 tsp.*
Capers	*2 tsp.*	*2 tsp.*	*2 tsp.*

Clean the trout and sprinkle inside with salt and pepper. Brush inside and outside the fish with melted butter. Mix the parsley and lemon rind and divide between the fish, placing inside each one. Put 2 fish into a cook-bag with the wine and secure loosely. Cook in the microwave oven for 3 minutes. Cut the bag carefully so that no liquid is spilt and pour the liquid into another cook-bag. Lift the cooked fish on to a warm serving dish. Put the remaining 2 fish into the liquid and tie the bag loosely. Microwave for 3 minutes. Pour the liquid into a bowl. Put the cooked fish on to the serving dish. Mix the cornflour with a little of the liquid and stir into the bowl. Heat in the microwave oven for 30 seconds, stir well and pour over the fish. Sprinkle with capers before serving.

SPECIAL INSTRUCTIONS
Freeze without capers. Add before serving.

REHEAT
25 minutes

Stuffed Plaice in Wine Sauce

* 1 month Serves 4

INGREDIENTS	Imperial	Metric	American
Plaice fillets (flounder)	*8*	*8*	*8*
Potted shrimps in butter	*4 oz.*	*100 g.*	*1/2 cup*
Dry white wine	*1/4 pt.*	*150 ml.*	*2/3 cup*
Water	*1/4 pt.*	*150 ml.*	*2/3 cup*
Lemon juice	*1/2 tsp.*	*1/2 tsp.*	*1/2 tsp.*
Bay leaf	*1*	*1*	*1*
Blade of mace	*1*	*1*	*1*
Salt and pepper			
Butter	*1/2 oz.*	*15 g.*	*1 tbsp.*
Plain flour	*1/2 oz.*	*15 g.*	*1 tbsp.*
Sprigs of watercress to garnish			

Skin the fish fillets. Divide the potted shrimps into eight portions and place one portion on each piece of fish. Roll up the fillets and place close together in a shallow dish. Mix together the wine, water and lemon juice and pour over the fish. Add the bay leaf, mace, salt and pepper. Cover with clingfilm and make two small holes in the film. Cook in the microwave oven for 5 minutes. Drain off the cooking liquid and reserve. Remove the bay leaf and mace, and keep the fish hot. Mix the butter and flour together in a bowl and pour in the cooking liquid, whisking well. Microwave for 1 minute, stir well and cook for 1 minute. Pour over the fish and garnish with watercress sprigs.

SPECIAL INSTRUCTIONS
Freeze without watercress, and add after reheating.

REHEAT
15 minutes

Trout with Almonds

✱ 1 month Serves 4

INGREDIENTS	Imperial	Metric	American
Trout	*4 × 8 oz.*	*4 × 225 g.*	*4 × 8 oz.*
Butter	*3 oz.*	*75 g.*	*6 tbsp.*
Flaked blanched almonds	*2 oz.*	*50 g.*	*½ cup*
Salt and pepper			
Lemon juice	*1½ tsp.*	*1½ tsp.*	*1½ tsp.*
Lemon	*1*	*1*	*1*
Watercress or parsley to garnish			

Clean the trout and arrange in a shallow dish. Put 2 oz./50 g./4 tablespoons butter into a bowl and heat in the microwave oven for 30 seconds. Add the almonds and heat for 3 minutes until lightly coloured. Keep on one side. Sprinkle the trout with salt, pepper and lemon juice, and put a piece of the remaining butter on each one. Cover with clingfilm and make two small holes in the film. Cook in the microwave oven for 9 minutes. Spoon over the almonds and microwave for 2 minutes. Leave to stand for 2 minutes before serving. Cut lemon into four wedges and serve one with each trout. Garnish with watercress or parsley.

REHEAT
25 minutes

Creole Prawns

* 1 month Serves 4

INGREDIENTS	Imperial	Metric	American
Oil	*3 tbsp.*	*3 tbsp.*	*3 tbsp.*
Onion	*1 large*	*1 large*	*1 large*
Green pepper	*1*	*1*	*1*
Celery sticks	*3*	*3*	*3*
Plain flour	*1 oz.*	*25 g.*	*2 tbsp.*
Salt and freshly ground black pepper			
Garlic clove	*1*	*1*	*1*
Concentrated tomato purée	*4 tbsp.*	*4 tbsp.*	*4 tbsp.*
Lemon juice	*1 tsp.*	*1 tsp.*	*1 tsp.*
Worcestershire sauce	*½ tsp.*	*½ tsp.*	*½ tsp.*
Tabasco sauce	*Few drops*	*Few drops*	*Few drops*
Bay leaf	*1*	*1*	*1*
Water	*½ pt.*	*300 ml.*	*1¼ cups*
Shelled prawns	*1 lb.*	*450 g.*	*1 lb.*

Put the oil into a casserole and heat in the microwave oven for 1 minute. Chop the onion, pepper and celery and stir into the oil. Cook for 5 minutes, stirring once. Mix in the flour, salt, pepper, crushed garlic, and heat for 1 minute. Add the tomato purée, lemon juice, sauces, bay leaf and water. Stir well and heat for 3 minutes until sauce bubbles. Add prawns and stir well. Cover and microwave for 6 minutes. Serve with rice or pasta.

REHEAT
15 minutes

Baked Crab

✱ 1 month Serves 4

INGREDIENTS	Imperial	Metric	American
Butter	*1 oz.*	*25 g.*	*2 tbsp.*
Onion	*1 small*	*1 small*	*1 small*
Dry sherry	*2 tbsp.*	*30 ml.*	*2 tbsp.*
Crabmeat (brown and white)	*8 oz.*	*225 g.*	*8 oz.*
Fresh white breadcrumbs	*½ oz.*	*15 g.*	*¼ cup*
Made mustard	*½ tsp.*	*½ tsp.*	*½ tsp.*
Worcestershire sauce	*½ tsp.*	*½ tsp.*	*½ tsp.*
Chopped fresh parsley	*1 tbsp.*	*1 tbsp.*	*1 tbsp.*
Salt and freshly ground black pepper			
Browned breadcrumbs	*1 oz.*	*25 g.*	*½ cup*
Grated Parmesan cheese	*1 tbsp.*	*1 tbsp.*	*1 tbsp.*
Lemon	*1*	*1*	*1*

Put the butter into a shallow dish and add the finely chopped onion. Microwave for 2 minutes. Stir in the sherry and microwave for 1 minute. Add the crabmeat, breadcrumbs, mustard, Worcestershire sauce, parsley and seasoning. Cook in the microwave oven for 3 minutes. Mix the browned breadcrumbs and cheese together and sprinkle on top of the crab. Microwave for 2 minutes. Serve immediately, garnished with lemon cut into wedges.

SPECIAL INSTRUCTIONS
Freeze without breadcrumbs and cheese topping. Add before reheating.

REHEAT
10 minutes

Salmon Loaf

* 1 month Serves 4

INGREDIENTS	Imperial	Metric	American
Canned pink or red salmon	*1 lb.*	*450 g.*	*1 lb.*
Lemon juice	*1 tbsp.*	*1 tbsp.*	*1 tbsp.*
Milk	*¼ pt.*	*150 ml.*	*⅔ cup*
Fresh white breadcrumbs	*3 oz.*	*75 g.*	*1½ cups*
Egg	*1*	*1*	*1*
Salt and pepper			
Chopped fresh parsley	*1 tbsp.*	*1 tbsp.*	*1 tbsp.*
Butter	*1 oz.*	*25 g.*	*2 tbsp.*

Put the salmon and its liquid into a bowl. Remove any bones and skin. Mash the salmon with a fork and work in all the other ingredients except the butter. Put the butter into a rectangular dish and heat in the microwave oven for 30 seconds. Add the melted butter to the salmon mixture, and grease the dish with any remaining butter. Put the salmon mixture into the dish. Cook in the microwave oven for 8 minutes. Leave to stand for 5 minutes. Serve hot or cold with vegetables or salad.

THAW
At room temperature 3 hours
OR
REHEAT
15 minutes

Seafood Curry

✱ 1 month Serves 4

INGREDIENTS	Imperial	Metric	American
Butter	*2 oz.*	*50 g.*	*4 tbsp.*
Onion	*1 large*	*1 large*	*1 large*
Eating apple	*1 medium*	*1 medium*	*1 medium*
Plain flour	*1 oz.*	*25 g.*	*2 tbsp.*
Curry powder	*1½ tsp.*	*1½ tsp.*	*1½ tsp.*
Salt and freshly ground black pepper			
Pinch of sugar			
Lemon juice	*½ tsp.*	*½ tsp.*	*½ tsp.*
Chicken stock	*¾ pt.*	*450 ml.*	*2 cups*
Peeled prawns	*1 lb.*	*450 g.*	*1 lb.*

Put the butter into a casserole. Chop the onion and add to the butter. Cook in the microwave oven for 5 minutes, stirring twice. Peel and chop the apple and add to the onion. Cook for 1 minute. Stir in the flour, curry powder, salt, pepper and sugar. Cover and cook for 1 minute. Stir in the lemon juice and hot chicken stock, stirring well. Microwave for 5 minutes, stirring four times during cooking. Add the prawns and heat for 3 minutes. Serve with rice.

REHEAT
15 minutes

MEAT

N.B. Although some meat dishes will look different from those cooked by other methods, their texture and flavour will not be affected in any way.

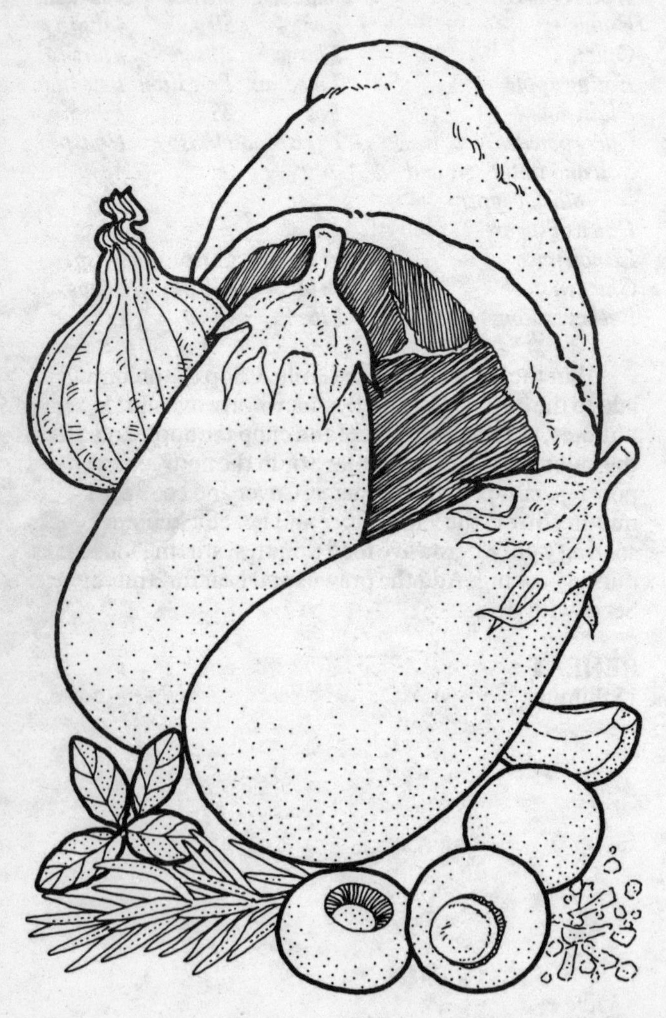

Pitta Pockets

* 2 months Serves 4

INGREDIENTS	Imperial	Metric	American
Butter	*1 oz.*	*25 g.*	*2 tbsp.*
Onion	*1 medium*	*1 medium*	*1 medium*
Raw minced beef	*8 oz.*	*25 g.*	*8 oz.*
Garlic clove	*1*	*1*	*1*
Canned tomatoes	*4 oz.*	*100 g.*	*4 oz.*
Paprika	*1 tsp.*	*1 tsp.*	*1 tsp.*
Worcestershire sauce	*1 tsp.*	*1 tsp.*	*1 tsp.*
Chopped fresh parsley	*2 tsp.*	*2 tsp.*	*2 tsp.*
Salt and pepper			
Pitta breads	*4*	*4*	*4*

Put the butter into a shallow dish. Chop the onion finely. Add to the butter and cook in the microwave oven for 3 minutes. Add the beef and continue cooking for 5 minutes, stirring twice. Add the crushed garlic, tomatoes and their juice, paprika, Worcestershire sauce, parsley, salt and pepper. Cover and microwave for 2 minutes. Leave to stand while preparing the bread. Wrap each pitta bread in greaseproof paper and microwave for 20 seconds. Fill each pitta bread pocket with some of the meat mixture and serve at once with salad.

SPECIAL INSTRUCTIONS
Freeze meat filling only. Heat pitta bread as instructed and fill with hot meat.

REHEAT
8 minutes

Burgundy Beef

✻ 2 months Serves 4

INGREDIENTS	Imperial	Metric	American
Streaky bacon rashers	*4*	*4*	*4*
Onion	*1 medium*	*1 medium*	*1 medium*
Chuck steak	*1 lb.*	*450 g.*	*1 lb.*
Beef stock	*½ pt.*	*300 ml.*	*1¼ cups*
Red wine	*¼ pt.*	*150 ml.*	*⅔ cup*
Sprig of parsley			
Sprig of thyme			
Bay leaf	*1*	*1*	*1*
Garlic clove	*1*	*1*	*1*
Salt and freshly ground black pepper			
Button onions	*8*	*8*	*8*
Button mushrooms	*4 oz.*	*100 g.*	*4 oz.*
Chopped fresh parsley	*1 tbsp.*	*1 tbsp.*	*1 tbsp.*

Remove the rind from the bacon and cut into small strips. Chop the onion finely. Put bacon and onion into a casserole dish and cook in the microwave oven for 4 minutes, stirring twice. Cut the steak into cubes and add to the casserole dish. Microwave for 2 minutes. Add the stock, wine, herbs, crushed garlic, salt and pepper. Microwave for 10 minutes, stirring once. Peel the button onions and leave whole. Add to the meat and continue cooking for 20 minutes, stirring twice. Add the mushrooms, stir well and cook for 5 minutes. Leave to stand for 5 minutes before stirring, and garnish with chopped parsley.

SPECIAL INSTRUCTIONS
Freeze without parsley. Garnish after reheating.

REHEAT
20 minutes

Beef Olives

* 2 months   Serves 4

INGREDIENTS	Imperial	Metric	American
Topside beef (top round)	*1 lb.*	*450 g.*	*1 lb.*
Onion	*1 small*	*1 small*	*1 small*
Button mushrooms	*2 oz.*	*50 g.*	*½ cup*
Fresh white breadcrumbs	*1 oz.*	*25 g.*	*½ cup*
Grated lemon rind	*1 tsp.*	*1 tsp.*	*1 tsp.*
Lemon juice	*1 tbsp.*	*15 ml.*	*1 tbsp.*
Egg	*1*	*1*	*1*
Mixed herbs	*1–2 tsp.*	*1–2 tsp.*	*1–2 tsp.*
Butter	*1 oz.*	*25 g.*	*2 tbsp.*
Plain flour	*1 oz.*	*25 g.*	*2 tbsp.*
Beef stock	*¾ pt.*	*450 ml.*	*2 cups*
Salt and freshly ground black pepper			
Chopped fresh parsley	*1 tbsp.*	*1 tbsp.*	*1 tbsp.*

Cut the meat into 6–8 thin slices. Chop the onion and mushrooms very finely. Mix with the breadcrumbs, lemon rind and juice, egg and herbs. Divide this mixture between the beef slices and form into parcels. Tie with cotton or thin string. Put the butter into an oblong casserole dish and melt in the microwave oven for 1 minute. Stir in the flour and add the stock and seasoning. Cook in the microwave oven for 2 minutes. Arrange the beef parcels in a single layer in the dish and cook in the microwave oven for 15 minutes, turning the beef parcels every three minutes. Leave to stand for 5 minutes before serving and sprinkle with parsley.

SPECIAL INSTRUCTIONS
Freeze without parsley. Garnish after reheating.

REHEAT
20 minutes

Beef Curry

✱ 2 months Serves 4

INGREDIENTS	Imperial	Metric	American
Topside beef (top round)	*1 lb.*	*450 g.*	*1 lb.*
Onion	*1 large*	*1 large*	*1 large*
Garlic cloves	2	2	2
Mild curry powder	*2 tbsp.*	*2 tbsp.*	*2 tbsp.*
Ground ginger	*½ tsp.*	*½ tsp.*	*½ tsp.*
Ground coriander	*½ tsp.*	*½ tsp.*	*½ tsp.*
Wine vinegar	*6 tbsp.*	*90 ml.*	*6 tbsp.*
Water	*½ pt.*	*300 ml.*	*1¼ cups*
Oil	*2 tbsp.*	*30 ml.*	*2 tbsp.*
Curry paste	*1 tsp.*	*1 tsp.*	*1 tsp.*
Salt and pepper			
Coconut	*1 tbsp.*	*1 tbsp.*	*1 tbsp.*
Boiling water	*¼ pt.*	*150 ml.*	*¾ cup*

Cut the beef into 1 in./2.5 cm. cubes. Infuse the coconut in the boiling water for one hour. Chop the onion finely. Crush the garlic and mix with the curry powder, ginger, coriander and vinegar. Add the onion and then stir in the beef cubes. Cover and leave in the refrigerator for at least 2 hours. Put the water and oil into a casserole and heat in the microwave oven for 2 minutes. Stir in the beef, onion and all the juices, and add salt and pepper. Strain the coconut milk and add the liquid. Cover and microwave for 15 minutes. Stir well and leave to stand for 10 minutes. Stir in the curry paste and microwave again for 15 minutes. Leave to stand for 3 minutes before serving with rice and chutney.

REHEAT
20 minutes

Goulash

✱ 2 months Serves 4

INGREDIENTS	Imperial	Metric	American
Butter	*1 oz.*	*25 g.*	*2 tbsp.*
Oil	*1 tbsp.*	*15 ml.*	*1 tbsp.*
Onion	*1 large*	*1 large*	*1 large*
Topside beef (top round)	*1 lb.*	*450 g.*	*1 lb.*
Concentrated tomato purée	*6 tbsp.*	*6 tbsp.*	*6 tbsp.*
Canned tomatoes	*8 oz.*	*225 g.*	*8 oz.*
Beef stock	*½ pt.*	*300 ml.*	*1¼ cups*
Plain flour	*1 oz.*	*25 g.*	*2 tbsp.*
Paprika	*½ oz.*	*15 g.*	*1 tbsp.*
Salt and pepper			
Natural yoghurt	*3 tbsp.*	*45 ml.*	*3 tbsp.*

Put the butter and oil into a casserole. Heat in the microwave oven for 1 minute. Add the thinly sliced onion. Microwave for 5 minutes. Cut the beef into 1 in./2.5 cm. cubes and add to the onion. Microwave for 2 minutes, stirring once. Stir in the tomato purée and canned tomatoes with their juice. Reserve 3 tablespoons beef stock, and stir the rest into the meat. Mix the flour and paprika with the reserved stock and stir into the meat until well mixed. Season well, stir and microwave for 15 minutes, stirring 5 times during cooking. Cover and leave to stand for 5 minutes. Pour in natural yoghurt just before serving. Serve with rice or boiled potatoes.

SPECIAL INSTRUCTIONS
Freeze without yoghurt. Add after reheating.

REHEAT
20 minutes

Meat Balls in Tomato Sauce

* 2 months Serves 4

INGREDIENTS	Imperial	Metric	American
Onion	*1 medium*	*1 medium*	*1 medium*
Butter	*2 oz.*	*50 g.*	*4 tbsp.*
Raw minced beef	*1 lb.*	*450 g.*	*1 lb.*
Fresh white breadcrumbs	*1 oz.*	*25 g.*	*½ cup*
Mixed herbs	*½ tsp.*	*½ tsp.*	*½ tsp.*
Egg	*1*	*1*	*1*
Salt and pepper			
Plain flour	*1 oz.*	*25 g.*	*2 tbsp.*
Concentrated tomato purée	*2 tbsp.*	*2 tbsp.*	*2 tbsp.*
Canned tomatoes	*8 oz.*	*225 g.*	*8 oz.*
Beef stock	*½ pt.*	*300 ml.*	*1¼ cups*

Chop the onion very finely. Put 1 oz./25 g./2 tablespoons butter into a shallow dish and microwave for 2 minutes. Add the onion to the butter with the beef, breadcrumbs, herbs, egg, salt and pepper. Stir well and then shape into 16 balls. Put the remaining butter into the dish and melt in the microwave oven for 1 minute. Arrange the meatballs in the butter and turn them so that they are coated in fat. Microwave for 5 minutes, turning the meatballs once. Lift out the meatballs and keep on one side. Work the flour into the fat and then mix in the tomato purée. Put the tomatoes and their juice through a sieve to get rid of the pips. Stir into the flour. Add the beef stock. Return to microwave and cook for 3 minutes, stirring twice. Add the meatballs, stir well and microwave for 8 minutes, turning the meatballs four times. Serve with pasta, rice or mashed potatoes.

REHEAT
20 minutes

Gingered Lamb Chops

* 2 months Serves 4

INGREDIENTS	Imperial	Metric	American
Lamb chump chops	*4*	*4*	*4*
Butter	*2 oz.*	*50 g.*	*4 tbsp.*
Lemon juice	*1 tbsp.*	*15 ml.*	*1 tbsp.*
Grated lemon rind	*2 tsp.*	*2 tsp.*	*2 tsp.*
Ground ginger	*1 tsp.*	*1 tsp.*	*1 tsp.*
Garlic clove	*½*	*½*	*½*
Salt and pepper			

Put the chops into a shallow dish. Put the butter into a bowl and melt in the microwave oven for 1 minute. Add the lemon juice and rind, ginger, crushed garlic and seasoning and mix well. Spread on both sides of the chops. Cook in the microwave oven for 12 minutes, turning the chops three times during cooking. Serve with vegetables or a salad.

REHEAT
10 minutes

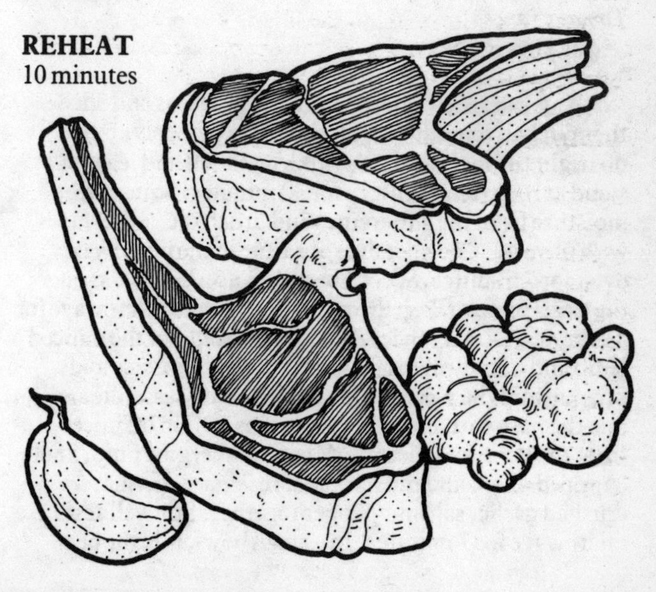

Lamb and Aubergine Casserole

* 2 months Serves 4–6

INGREDIENTS	Imperial	Metric	American
Aubergines	*4 medium*	*4 medium*	*4 medium*
Salt	*1 tbsp.*	*1 tbsp.*	*1 tbsp.*
Olive oil	*2 tbsp.*	*30 ml.*	*2 tbsp.*
Shoulder lamb, minced	*2 lb.*	*1 kg.*	*2 lb.*
Onion	*1 large*	*1 large*	*1 large*
Button mushrooms	*8 oz.*	*225 g.*	*8 oz.*
Rosemary	*1 tsp.*	*1 tsp.*	*1 tsp.*
Thyme	*½ tsp.*	*½ tsp.*	*½ tsp.*
Garlic clove	*1*	*1*	*1*
Beef stock	*¼ pt.*	*300 ml.*	*⅔ cup*
Cornflour	*1 tsp.*	*1 tsp.*	*1 tsp.*
Concentrated tomato purée	*2 tbsp.*	*2 tbsp.*	*2 tbsp.*
Eggs	*3*	*3*	*3*
Salt and pepper			
Tomato Sauce (see page 117)			

Cut the green caps from the aubergines and slice them in half lengthwise. Slash the pulp deeply, but not right through skins. Sprinkle with salt and leave to stand at room temperature for 30 minutes. Squeeze the moisture from the aubergines and brush the cut surfaces with olive oil. Cook 4 halves at a time in the microwave oven for 7 minutes. Scoop the pulp into a bowl, keeping the skins intact. Chop the pulp coarsely and microwave for 4 minutes, stirring twice. In another bowl put the minced lamb and microwave for 7 minutes, stirring twice and breaking up the pieces of meat. Oil a deep casserole and line the base with the aubergine skins. Drain off juices from the lamb and discard. Mix the aubergine pulp, finely chopped onion and mushrooms, rosemary, thyme, crushed garlic, salt and pepper together. Stir well and microwave for 7 minutes. In a small bowl, mix the beef stock and cornflour until smooth and microwave for 1 minute, stirring twice. Stir into the lamb mixture with the tomato purée and eggs. Pour into the casserole and fold the ends of the aubergine skins over the filling. Cover and microwave for 11 minutes. Turn out on a flat serving plate and serve with hot tomato sauce.

REHEAT
20 minutes

Meat Loaf

* 2 months Serves 4

INGREDIENTS	Imperial	Metric	American
Butter	*1 oz.*	*25 g.*	*2 tbsp.*
Onion	*1 medium*	*1 medium*	*1 medium*
Raw minced beef	*8 oz.*	*225 g.*	*8 oz.*
Pork sausagemeat	*8 oz.*	*225 g.*	*8 oz.*
Mixed herbs	*1–2 tsp.*	*1–2 tsp.*	*1–2 tsp.*
Tomato ketchup	*1 tbsp.*	*1 tbsp.*	*1 tbsp.*
Porridge oats	*1 tbsp.*	*1 tbsp.*	*1 tbsp.*
Salt and freshly ground black pepper			

Put the butter into a bowl with the finely chopped onion. Cook in the microwave oven for 4 minutes, stirring once. Stir in the beef, sausagemeat, herbs, ketchup, oats and seasoning, mixing very thoroughly so that the meats are well mixed. Put into a microwave loaf dish and cook for 7 minutes. Leave to stand for 5 minutes before serving hot. The meat loaf is also very good cold with salad, or used as a sandwich filling.

REHEAT
20 minutes

Pork in Cider Sauce

✱ 2 months Serves 4

INGREDIENTS	Imperial	Metric	American
Butter	*1 oz.*	*25 g.*	*2 tbsp.*
Onion	*1 medium*	*1 medium*	*1 medium*
Pork tenderloin	*1 lb.*	*450 g.*	*1 lb.*
Mixed herbs	*½ tsp.*	*½ tsp.*	*½ tsp.*
Button mushrooms	*4 oz.*	*100 g.*	*4 oz.*
Dry cider	*¼ pt.*	*150 ml.*	*⅔ cup*
Salt and pepper			
Single cream	*¼ pt.*	*150 ml.*	*⅔ cup*
Chopped fresh parsley	*1 tbsp.*	*1 tbsp.*	*1 tbsp.*

Put the butter into a casserole dish. Add the finely chopped onion and cook in the microwave oven for 4 minutes. Cut the tenderloin across in thin rounds and add to the dish. Microwave for 2 minutes, stirring once. Add the herbs, sliced mushrooms, cider, salt and pepper. Cook in the microwave oven for 7 minutes, stirring twice. Stir in the cream and microwave for 2 minutes, stirring once. Sprinkle with chopped parsley before serving.

SPECIAL INSTRUCTIONS
Freeze without cream and parsley. Add just before serving.

REHEAT
15 minutes

Oriental Pork

* 2 months Serves 4

INGREDIENTS	Imperial	Metric	American
Oil	*1 tbsp.*	*15 ml.*	*1 tbsp.*
Onion	*1 medium*	*1 medium*	*1 medium*
Carrot	*1 medium*	*1 medium*	*1 medium*
Green pepper	*1 medium*	*1 medium*	*1 medium*
Celery stick	*1*	*1*	*1*
Lean pork	*1 lb.*	*450 g.*	*1 lb.*
Canned tomatoes	*1 lb.*	*450 g.*	*1 lb.*
Concentrated tomato purée	*1 tbsp.*	*1 tbsp.*	*1 tbsp.*
Vinegar	*2 tbsp.*	*30 ml.*	*2 tbsp.*
Light soft brown sugar	*½ oz.*	*15 g.*	*1 tbsp.*
Chicken stock	*½ pt.*	*300 ml.*	*1¼ cups*
Plum jam	*1 tbsp.*	*1 tbsp.*	*1 tbsp.*
Salt and pepper			
Cornflour	*2 tsp.*	*2 tsp.*	*2 tsp.*

Put the oil into a casserole. Chop the onion finely. Cut the carrot and green pepper into thin strips. Slice the celery thinly. Put into the oil and cook in the microwave oven for 5 minutes, stirring twice. Cut the pork in cubes and add to the vegetables. Cook in the microwave oven for 2 minutes. Put the tomatoes and their juice through a sieve to get rid of the pips. Pour over the meat and stir in the purée, vinegar, sugar, stock, jam and seasoning. Cover and microwave for 20 minutes, stirring twice. Mix the cornflour with a little water and stir into the casserole. Microwave for 2 minutes, stirring twice. Leave to stand for 10 minutes.

REHEAT
15 minutes

Sausage and Apple Bake

∗ 1 month Serves 4

INGREDIENTS	Imperial	Metric	American
Pork sausages	*1 lb.*	*450 g.*	*1 lb.*
Onions	*2 large*	*2 large*	*2 large*
Eating apples	2	2	2
Barbecue Sauce *(see page 119)*			

Put the sausages into a shallow dish and prick well. Cover with clingfilm and make two small holes in the film. Cook in the microwave oven for 6 minutes. Take out the sausages and keep warm. Slice the onions thinly and put into the sausage fat. Cover and cook for 6 minutes. Peel the apples and cut into thin slices. Add the sausages and apples to the onions and heat for 3 minutes. Pour on the sauce and continue cooking for 4 minutes. Serve with hot crusty bread and green salad.

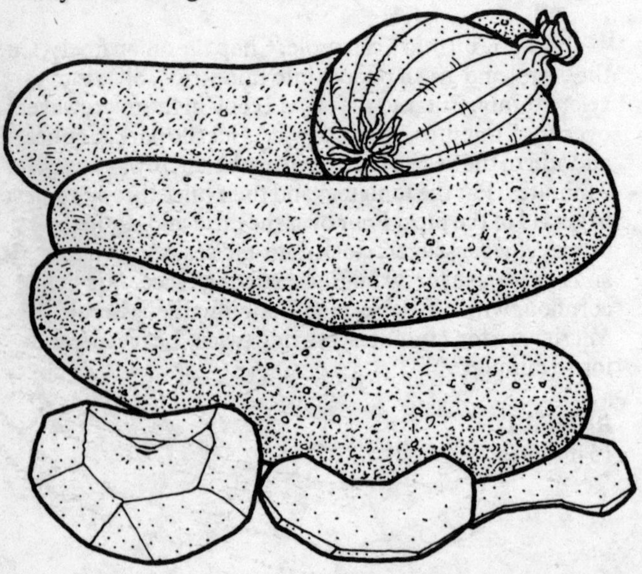

Apple Gammon

* 1 month Serves 4

INGREDIENTS	Imperial	Metric	American
Gammon steaks	*4 × 6 oz.*	*4 × 175 g.*	*4 × 6 oz.*
Onion	*1 medium*	*1 medium*	*1 medium*
Dry cider	*½ pt.*	*300 ml.*	*1¼ cups*
Eating apple	*1*	*1*	*1*
Sage leaves	2	2	2
Salt and pepper			

Remove the rind from the gammon steaks. Put the steaks in a casserole in a single layer and cook in the microwave oven for 6 minutes, turning once. Chop the onion finely and add to the dish. Microwave for 3 minutes. Add the cider. Peel and core the apple and cut in thin slices. Add to the dish with the finely chopped sage leaves, salt and pepper. Microwave for 7 minutes, stirring twice. Leave to stand for 5 minutes before serving.

REHEAT
20 minutes

Herbed Liver

✱ 2 months Serves 4

INGREDIENTS	Imperial	Metric	American
Lambs' liver	*12 oz.*	*350 g.*	*12 oz.*
Onion	*1 medium*	*1 medium*	*1 medium*
Streaky bacon rashers	*2*	*2*	*2*
Butter	*1 oz.*	*25 g.*	*2 tbsp.*
Oil	*1 tbsp.*	*15 ml.*	*1 tbsp.*
Canned tomatoes	*1 lb.*	*450 g.*	*1 lb.*
Mixed herbs	*½ tsp.*	*½ tsp.*	*½ tsp.*
Salt and pepper			

Cut the liver in thin slices. Chop the onion and bacon. Put the butter and oil in a casserole and heat in the microwave oven for 2 minutes. Add the onion and bacon and continue cooking for 3 minutes, stirring once. Add the liver and cook for 1 minute. Sieve the tomatoes to get rid of the pips. Pour over the liver and stir in the herbs and seasoning. Continue cooking for 7 minutes, stirring twice. Leave to stand for 5 minutes before serving.

REHEAT
15 minutes

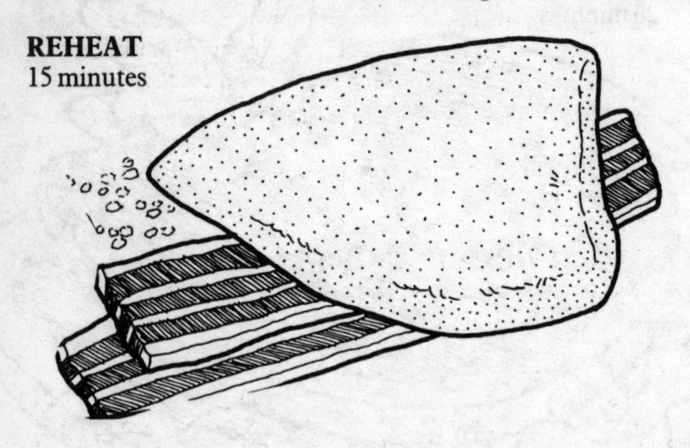

Kidneys in Red Wine

✱ 2 months Serves 4

INGREDIENTS	Imperial	Metric	American
Onion	*1 small*	*1 small*	*1 small*
Button mushrooms	*4 oz.*	*100 g.*	*4 oz.*
Butter	*1½ oz.*	*40 g.*	*3 tbsp.*
Lambs' kidneys	*10*	*10*	*10*
Plain flour	*½ oz.*	*15 g.*	*1 tbsp.*
Red wine	*¼ pt.*	*150 ml.*	*⅔ cup*
Beef stock	*4 tbsp.*	*60 ml.*	*4 tbsp.*
Made mustard	*1 tsp.*	*1 tsp.*	*1 tsp.*
Salt and pepper			
Chopped fresh parsley	*1 tbsp.*	*1 tbsp.*	*1 tbsp.*

Chop the onion finely and slice the mushrooms. Put the onion and butter into a shallow dish and cook in the microwave oven for 4 minutes, stirring once. Add the mushrooms, and cook for 1 minute. Skin the kidneys, cut them in half lengthwise. Cut out the white core from each half. Add to the onion and cook for 5 minutes, stirring once. Stir in the flour, and then the wine, stock and mustard, and season with salt and pepper. Mix well and microwave for 8 minutes. Leave to stand for 5 minutes. Serve sprinkled with parsley.

REHEAT
15 minutes

SPECIAL INSTRUCTIONS
Freeze without parsley. Garnish after reheating.

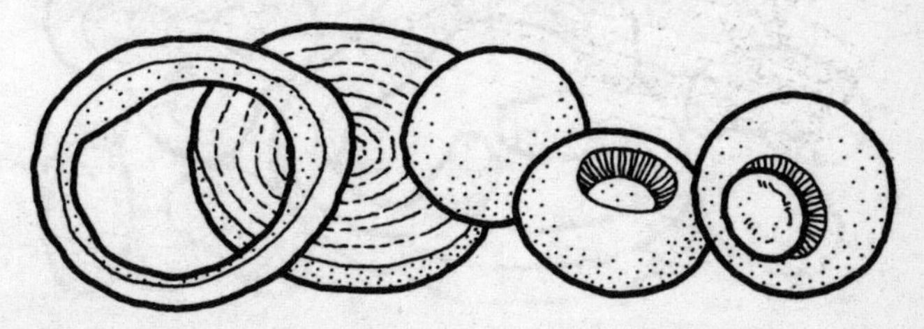

Chilli Con Carne

∗ 2 months Serves 4

INGREDIENTS	Imperial	Metric	American
Oil	*1 tbsp.*	*15 ml.*	*1 tbsp.*
Onion	*1 medium*	*1 medium*	*1 medium*
Green pepper	*1 medium*	*1 medium*	*1 medium*
Garlic clove	*1*	*1*	*1*
Raw minced beef	*1 lb.*	*450 g.*	*1 lb.*
Canned tomatoes	*8 oz.*	*225 g.*	*8 oz.*
Beef stock	*½ pt.*	*300 ml.*	*1¼ cups*
Concentrated tomato purée	*2 tbsp.*	*2 tbsp.*	*2 tbsp.*
Chilli powder	*1–2 tbsp.*	*1–2 tbsp.*	*1–2 tbsp.*
Sugar	*½ tsp.*	*½ tsp.*	*½ tsp.*
Pinch of cumin			
Salt and pepper			
Canned kidney beans	*10 oz.*	*300 g.*	*10 oz.*

Put the oil into a casserole dish. Chop the onion and pepper finely and add to the oil. Cook in the microwave oven for 5 minutes, stirring once. Add the crushed garlic and the beef, mix well, and cook for 5 minutes. Stir in the tomatoes and their juice, stock, purée, chilli powder, sugar, cumin, salt and pepper. Mix well, cover and cook for 25 minutes, stirring three times during cooking. Drain the beans and stir into the meat. Cook for 2 minutes and serve with rice or crusty brown bread.

REHEAT
20 minutes

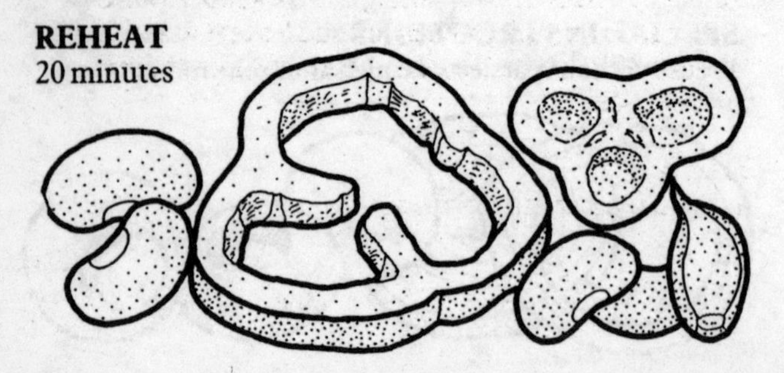

Ham and Cheese Loaf

✳ 1 month Serves 4

INGREDIENTS	Imperial	Metric	American
Milk	*¼ pt.*	*150 ml.*	*⅔ cup*
Egg	*1*	*1*	*1*
Tomato ketchup	*1 tbsp.*	*1 tbsp.*	*1 tbsp.*
Made mustard	*2 tsp.*	*2 tsp.*	*2 tsp.*
Salt and pepper			
Fresh white breadcrumbs	*2 oz.*	*50 g.*	*1 cup*
Lean cooked ham	*12 oz.*	*350 g.*	*3 cups*
Pork sausagemeat	*8 oz.*	*225 g.*	*8 oz.*
Grated onion	*1 tbsp.*	*1 tbsp.*	*1 tbsp.*
Cheddar cheese	*8 oz.*	*225 g.*	*8 oz.*
Glaze			
Tomato ketchup	*4 tbsp.*	*4 tbsp.*	*4 tbsp.*
Dark soft brown sugar	*1 oz.*	*25 g.*	*2 tbsp.*

Mix together the milk, egg, tomato ketchup, mustard, salt and pepper. Stir in the breadcrumbs. Add minced ham, sausagemeat and onion. Mix well. Cut the cheese into thin slices. Put one-third of the meat mixture into a microwave loaf dish. Put half the cheese slices on top. Add a second layer of meat mixture, remaining cheese slices and a final layer of meat mixture. Mix the ketchup and sugar together to make a glaze, and brush the top of the meat with half of it. Cook in microwave oven for 10 minutes. Brush with remaining glaze and microwave 10 minutes. Cover with kitchen foil and leave to stand for 15 minutes. Uncover and cool completely. Slice and serve cold with salad.

THAW
At room temperature 3 hours

POULTRY

N.B. Although some poultry dishes will look different from those cooked by other methods, their texture and flavour will not be affected in any way.

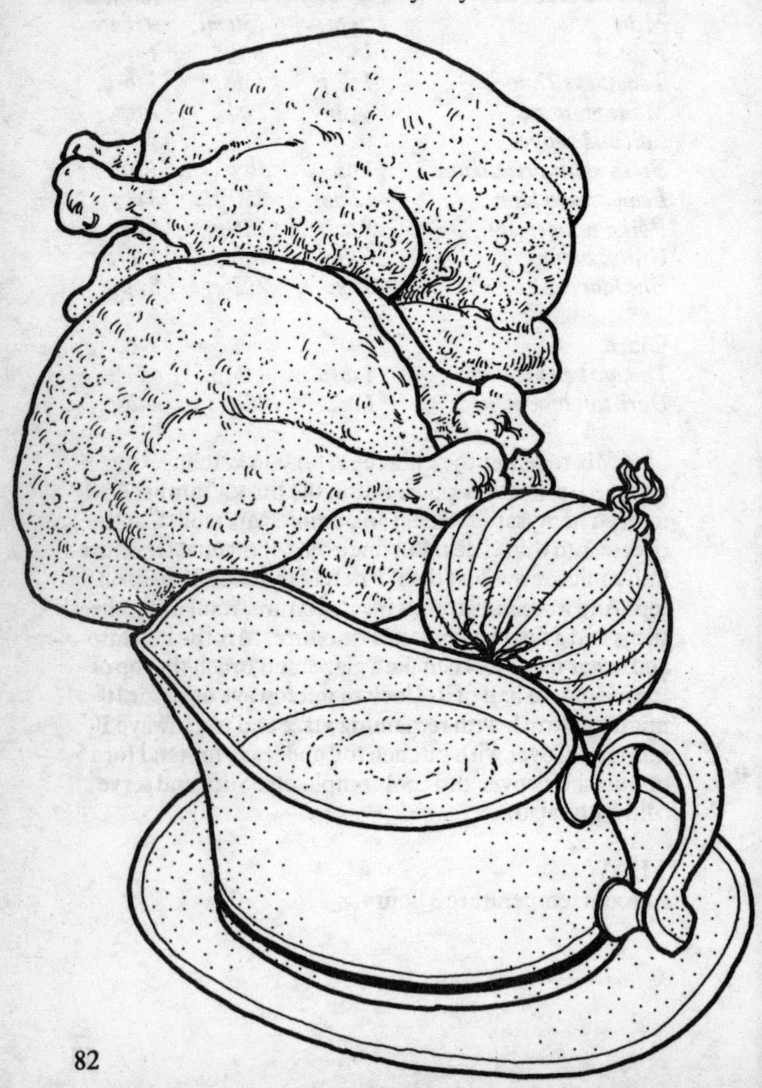

Italian Chicken

* 2 months Serves 4

INGREDIENTS	Imperial	Metric	American
Chicken joints	*4*	*4*	*4*
Onion	*1 small*	*1 small*	*1 small*
Garlic clove	*1*	*1*	*1*
Oil	*1 tbsp.*	*15 ml.*	*1 tbsp.*
Canned tomatoes	*1 lb.*	*450 g.*	*1 lb.*
Concentrated tomato purée	*4 tbsp.*	*4 tbsp.*	*4 tbsp.*
Sugar	*1 tsp.*	*1 tsp.*	*1 tsp.*
Fresh marjoram	*1 tsp.*	*1 tsp.*	*1 tsp.*
Fresh thyme	*½ tsp.*	*½ tsp.*	*½ tsp.*
Chopped fresh parsley	*2 tsp.*	*2 tsp.*	*2 tsp.*
Red wine	*¼ pt.*	*150 ml.*	*⅔ cup*
Salt and pepper			
Button mushrooms	*4 oz.*	*100 g.*	*4 oz.*

Chop the onion finely and crush the garlic. Put into a casserole dish with the oil and cook in the microwave oven for 4 minutes, stirring twice. Add the tomatoes and their juice, purée, sugar, herbs, wine, salt and pepper. Add the chicken pieces and make sure that they are covered with the other ingredients. Cover and cook in the microwave oven for 20 minutes. Slice the mushrooms and stir into the casserole. Microwave for 10 minutes without a cover, stirring the sauce twice. Cover and leave to stand for 10 minutes before serving with rice or pasta.

REHEAT
15 minutes

Herbed Lemon Chicken

✱ 2 months Serves 4

INGREDIENTS	Imperial	Metric	American
Chicken boneless breasts	*4*	*4*	*4*
Savoury sauce	*1 tbsp.*	*15 ml.*	*1 tbsp.*
Garlic clove	*1*	*1*	*1*
Fresh thyme	*1 tsp.*	*1 tsp.*	*1 tsp.*
Fresh marjoram	*1 tsp.*	*1 tsp.*	*1 tsp.*
Grated lemon rind	*2 tsp.*	*2 tsp.*	*2 tsp.*
Lemon juice	*5 tbsp.*	*75 ml.*	*5 tbsp.*
Water	*7 tbsp.*	*100 ml.*	*7 tbsp.*
Salt and pepper			
Pinch of paprika			
Chopped fresh parsley	*1 tbsp.*	*1 tbsp.*	*1 tbsp.*

Cut the chicken in cubes and put into a bowl with the savoury sauce. Toss lightly. Put into a shallow dish with the crushed garlic, herbs and lemon rind. Mix the lemon juice and water, and season with salt and pepper. Pour over the chicken. Sprinkle with paprika. Cover with clingfilm and make two small holes in the film. Microwave for 14 minutes, stirring twice. Leave to stand covered for 3 minutes. Sprinkle with parsley before serving.

SPECIAL INSTRUCTIONS
Freeze without parsley. Garnish after reheating.

REHEAT
15 minutes

Chicken Curry

* 2 months Serves 4

INGREDIENTS	Imperial	Metric	American
Chicken	*3 lb.*	*1.5 kg.*	*3 lb.*
Oil	*1 tbsp.*	*1 tbsp.*	*1 tbsp.*
Onions	*2 large*	*2 large*	*2 large*
Green pepper	*1*	*1*	*1*
Garlic cloves	*2*	*2*	*2*
Curry powder	*1–2 tbsp.*	*1–2 tbsp.*	*1–2 tbsp.*
Ground allspice	*2 tsp.*	*2 tsp.*	*2 tsp.*
Ground ginger	*1 tsp.*	*1 tsp.*	*1 tsp.*
Salt and pepper			
Tomatoes	*3*	*3*	*3*
Chicken stock	*¾ pt.*	*450 ml.*	*2 cups*
Eating apple	*1*	*1*	*1*

Make sure that the chicken has completely defrosted if frozen. Cut it into eight pieces. Put the oil into a casserole. Slice the onion thinly, dice the green pepper and crush the garlic cloves. Add to the oil and cook in microwave oven for 5 minutes, stirring once. Mix the curry powder, allspice, ginger, salt and pepper and rub into the chicken pieces. Put the chicken into the casserole. Peel the tomatoes and cut them into slices. Add to the casserole with half the chicken stock. Cover and microwave for 12 minutes. Stir well and add remaining stock. Peel the apple and cut into thin slices. Add to the casserole and stir well. Cover and microwave for 12 minutes. Serve with rice and chutney.

REHEAT
20 minutes

Indian Chicken

* 2 months Serves 4

INGREDIENTS	Imperial	Metric	American
Chicken breasts	*4*	*4*	*4*
Natural yoghurt	*¼ pt.*	*150 ml.*	*⅔ cup*
Curry powder	*1–2 tsp.*	*1–2 tsp.*	*1–2 tsp.*
Ground ginger	*1–2 tsp.*	*1–2 tsp.*	*1–2 tsp.*
Ground cinnamon	*½–1 tsp.*	*½–1 tsp.*	*½–1 tsp.*
Garlic clove	*½*	*½*	*½*
Lemon juice	*2 tsp.*	*2 tsp.*	*2 tsp.*
Salt and pepper			

Remove skin from the chicken. Using a sharp knife, make slashes at 1 in./2.5 cm. intervals on the breasts. Mix the yoghurt with the curry powder, ginger, cinnamon, crushed garlic, lemon juice, salt and pepper. Spread all over the chicken, pressing down well. Cover with clingfilm and leave in the refrigerator for at least 2 hours. Put the chicken breasts into a shallow dish with any of the mixture which has run off them. Cook in the microwave oven for 5 minutes. Turn over the chicken breasts and microwave for 10 minutes, turning the chicken once more. Serve with rice and chutney.

REHEAT
15 minutes

Herbed Chicken Drumsticks

* 2 months Serves 4

INGREDIENTS	Imperial	Metric	American
Chicken drumsticks	*8*	*8*	*8*
Butter	*4 oz.*	*100 g.*	*½ cup*
Tarragon	*1 tsp.*	*1 tsp.*	*1 tsp.*
Chives	*2 tsp.*	*2 tsp.*	*2 tsp.*
Parsley	*2 tbsp.*	*2 tbsp.*	*2 tbsp.*
Salt and freshly ground black pepper			

Put the butter into a shallow dish and heat in the microwave oven for 1 minute. Add chopped herbs, salt and pepper, and mix well. Put in the drumsticks and coat them thoroughly in the butter. Cook in the microwave oven for 16 minutes, turning the drumsticks three times during cooking. Serve hot or cold with vegetables or salad.

THAW
At room temperature 3 hours
OR
REHEAT
20 minutes, turning three times

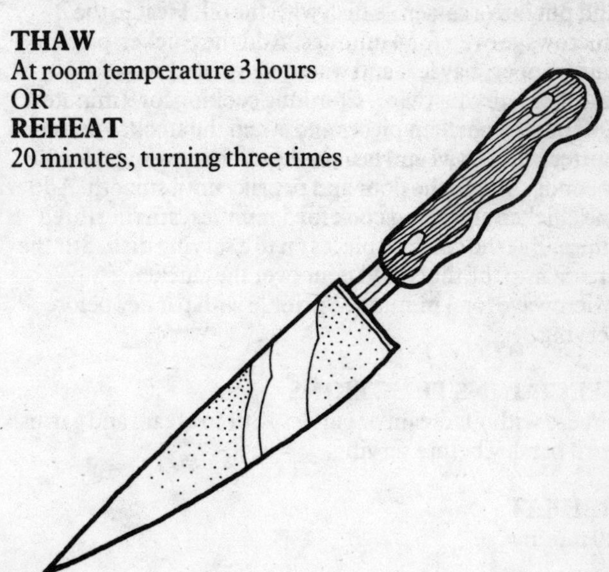

Creamed Chicken

* 2 months   Serves 4

INGREDIENTS	Imperial	Metric	American
Chicken	*3 lb.*	*1.5 kg.*	*3 lb.*
Onion	*1 medium*	*1 medium*	*1 medium*
Oil	*1 tbsp.*	*1 tbsp.*	*1 tbsp.*
Salt and pepper			
Bay leaf	*1*	*1*	*1*
Water	*1 pt.*	*600 ml.*	*2½ cups*
Butter	*1½ oz.*	*40 g.*	*3 tbsp.*
Plain flour	*1 oz.*	*25 g.*	*2 tbsp.*
Paprika	*1 tsp.*	*1 tsp.*	*1 tsp.*
Single cream	*¼ pt.*	*150 ml.*	*⅔ cup*
Chopped fresh parsley	*1 tbsp.*	*1 tbsp.*	*1 tbsp.*

Make sure that the chicken has completely defrosted if frozen, and cut it into eight pieces. Slice the onion thinly and put into a casserole dish with the oil. Heat in the microwave oven for 4 minutes. Add the chicken pieces, salt, pepper, bay leaf and water. Cover and cook for 10 minutes, stirring twice. Continue cooking for 9 minutes. Lift out the chicken pieces and strain the stock. Put the butter into a bowl and heat in the microwave oven for 30 seconds. Mix in the flour and paprika until smooth. Add the chicken stock and cook for 5 minutes, stirring three times. Put the chicken pieces on to a serving dish. Stir the cream into the sauce and pour over the chicken. Microwave for 4 minutes. Sprinkle with parsley before serving.

SPECIAL INSTRUCTIONS
Freeze without cream or parsley. Stir in cream and garnish with parsley before serving.

REHEAT
20 minutes

Chicken with Mushroom Sauce

* 2 months Serves 4

INGREDIENTS	Imperial	Metric	American
Chicken	*3 lb.*	*1.5 kg.*	*3 lb.*
Onion	*1 large*	*1 large*	*1 large*
Butter	*2 oz.*	*50 g.*	*4 tbsp.*
Button mushrooms	*8 oz.*	*225 g.*	*8 oz.*
Milk	*1 pt.*	*600 ml.*	*2½ cups*
Cornflour	*1 oz.*	*25 g.*	*2 tbsp.*
Salt and pepper			

Make sure that the chicken has completely defrosted if frozen, and the giblet bag removed. Chop the onion finely and put into a square casserole with half the butter. Cook in the microwave oven for 3 minutes. Place the chicken in the centre of the dish. Cover with clingfilm, and make two small holes in the film. Microwave for 24 minutes. Drain off any liquid and reserve. Leave casserole to stand with lid on while making the sauce. Put the remaining butter into a bowl and heat in the microwave oven for 30 seconds. Add sliced mushrooms. Cover and microwave for 2 minutes. Mix the cornflour with a little of the milk. Add the remaining milk to the mushrooms with the chicken cooking liquid. Microwave for 3 minutes, stirring twice. Stir in the cornflour mixture, salt and pepper. Microwave for 4 minutes, stirring twice. Carve the chicken and arrange on the serving dish with the onion. Pour over the mushroom sauce and serve at once.

SPECIAL INSTRUCTIONS
Carve chicken and pour over sauce before freezing.

REHEAT
20 minutes

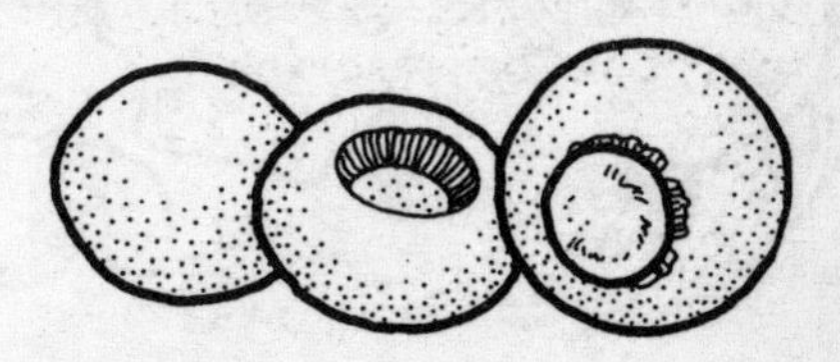

Chinese Chicken

✱ 2 months Serves 4

INGREDIENTS	Imperial	Metric	American
Chicken boneless breasts	*4*	*4*	*4*
Egg white	*1*	*1*	*1*
Cornflour	*½ oz.*	*15 g.*	*1 tbsp.*
Sugar	*½ tsp.*	*½ tsp.*	*½ tsp.*
Oil	*3 tbsp.*	*3 tbsp.*	*3 tbsp.*
Salted cashew nuts	*3 oz.*	*75 g.*	*¾ cup*
Ground ginger	*¼ tsp.*	*¼ tsp.*	*¼ tsp.*
Soy sauce	*1 tbsp.*	*15 ml.*	*1 tbsp.*
Dry sherry	*1 tbsp.*	*15 ml.*	*1 tbsp.*
Garlic powder	*¼ tsp.*	*¼ tsp.*	*¼ tsp.*

Cut the chicken into ½ in./1.25 cm. cubes. Beat the egg white lightly and mix with the cornflour and sugar. Stir in the chicken pieces and leave in the refrigerator for 30 minutes. Put 2 tablespoons oil into a shallow dish and heat in microwave oven for 1 minute. Lift chicken cubes from their dish with a slotted spoon and put into the oil. Microwave for 3 minutes. Put the remaining oil and nuts into a dish and microwave 2 minutes. Mix the nuts with the ginger, soy sauce, sherry and garlic. Stir in the chicken and microwave 1 minute. Serve with rice, or bean sprouts.

REHEAT
15 minutes

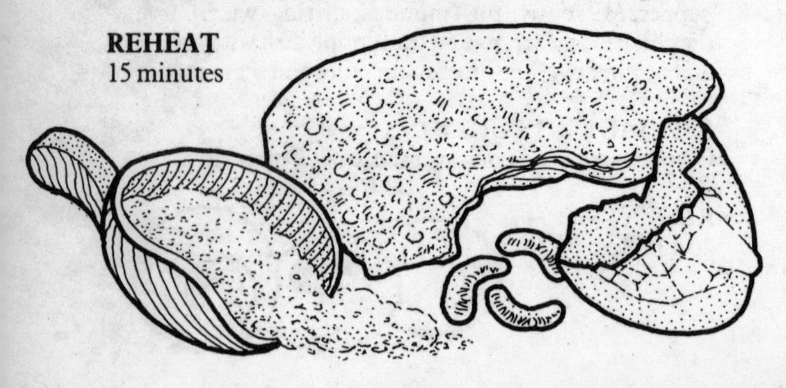

Orange Chicken

* 2 months Serves 4

INGREDIENTS	Imperial	Metric	American
Chicken joints	*4*	*4*	*4*
Unsweetened orange juice	*½ pt.*	*300 ml.*	*1¼ cups*
Garlic salt	*1 tsp.*	*1 tsp.*	*1 tsp.*
Pinch of paprika			
Chopped fresh parsley	*1 tbsp.*	*1 tbsp.*	*1 tbsp.*
Orange	*½*	*½*	*½*

Arrange the chicken pieces skin side up in a rectangular baking dish with the thicker pieces on the outside edge. Pour orange juice over the chicken. Sprinkle with garlic salt. Cover and cook in the microwave oven for 20 minutes, turning the chicken twice during cooking. Spoon over the orange juice two or three times and sprinkle the chicken with paprika. Cover and microwave for 3 minutes. Leave to stand covered for 5 minutes. Garnish with chopped parsley, and slices of fresh orange.

SPECIAL INSTRUCTIONS
Freeze without parsley. Garnish after reheating.

REHEAT
15 minutes

Turkey Bake

* 2 months Serves 4

INGREDIENTS	Imperial	Metric	American
Boneless turkey (or chicken) breasts	*1 lb.*	*450 g.*	*1 lb.*
Onion	*1 medium*	*1 medium*	*1 medium*
Oil	*2 tbsp.*	*30 ml.*	*2 tbsp.*
Plain flour	*1 oz.*	*25 g.*	*2 tbsp.*
Medium dry cider	*¾ pt.*	*450 ml.*	*2 cups*
Salt and pepper			
Canned red peppers	*4 oz.*	*100 g.*	*4 oz.*
Dry sherry	*2 tbsp.*	*30 ml.*	*2 tbsp.*
Double cream	*2 tbsp.*	*30 ml.*	*2 tbsp.*

Cut the turkey or chicken breasts into cubes. Chop the onion finely and put into a casserole dish with the oil. Heat in the microwave oven for 3 minutes. Stir in the pieces of turkey or chicken and cook for 5 minutes, stirring twice. Stir in the flour, mixing well. Microwave for 1 minute. Stir in the cider, mixing well until smooth, and season with salt and pepper. Cook in the microwave oven for 5 minutes, stirring twice. Cut the red peppers into strips and stir into the mixture. Microwave for 3 minutes, stirring once. Stir in the sherry and cream and serve at once with rice or pasta.

SPECIAL INSTRUCTIONS
Freeze without cream. Stir in after reheating.

REHEAT
15 minutes

Barbecued Chicken

* 2 months Serves 4

INGREDIENTS	Imperial	Metric	American
Chicken	*3 lb.*	*1.5 kg.*	*3 lb.*
Sauce			
Onion	*1 medium*	*1 medium*	*1 medium*
Butter	*1 oz.*	*25 g.*	*2 tbsp.*
Plain flour	*½ oz.*	*15 g.*	*1 tbsp.*
Made mustard	*2 tsp.*	*2 tsp.*	*2 tsp.*
Worcestershire sauce	*1 tbsp.*	*1 tbsp.*	*1 tbsp.*
Tabasco sauce	*1 tsp.*	*1 tsp.*	*1 tsp.*
Dark soft brown sugar	*½ oz.*	*15 g.*	*1 tbsp.*
Salt	*1 tsp.*	*1 tsp.*	*1 tsp.*
Vinegar	*1 tbsp.*	*1 tbsp.*	*1 tbsp.*
Tomato juice	*½ pt.*	*300 ml.*	*1¼ cups*

Make sure that the chicken has completely defrosted, and cut it into eight pieces.

To make the sauce chop the onion finely. Put into a bowl with the butter and cook in the microwave oven for 4 minutes. Stir in the flour and then all the remaining ingredients. Cook in the microwave oven for 2 minutes, stirring twice during cooking. Add the chicken pieces, stir well and cover. Microwave for 12 minutes. Stir again, cover and microwave for 10 minutes. Serve with crusty bread and green salad.

REHEAT
15 minutes

Herbed Chicken Livers

✱ 1 month Serves 4

INGREDIENTS	Imperial	Metric	American
Chicken livers	*1 lb.*	*450 g.*	*1 lb.*
Oil	*4 tbsp.*	*60 ml.*	*4 tbsp.*
Wine vinegar	*3 tbsp.*	*45 ml.*	*3 tbsp.*
Salt and freshly ground black pepper			
Dried basil	*1 tsp.*	*1 tsp.*	*1 tsp.*
Bay leaf	*1*	*1*	*1*
Butter	*1 oz.*	*25 g.*	*2 tbsp.*
Red pepper	*1*	*1*	*1*
Onion	*1 large*	*1 large*	*1 large*

Rinse the chicken livers and dry in kitchen paper. Put into a shallow dish. Mix the oil, vinegar, salt, plenty of pepper and herbs and pour over the chicken livers. Cover with clingfilm and leave in the refrigerator for 2 hours. Put the butter into a shallow dish and heat in the microwave oven for 1 minute. Add the pepper and onion cut in thin slices and cook for 5 minutes, stirring once. Drain the liquid from the livers and reserve. Add the livers to the pepper and onion and microwave for 5 minutes, stirring once. Remove the bay leaf from the liquid, and pour the liquid over the livers. Cook for 5 minutes, stirring once. Stir well before serving. Serve on toast or with rice.

REHEAT
15 minutes

Sweet and Sour Turkey

* 2 months Serves 4

INGREDIENTS	Imperial	Metric	American
Canned pineapple	*1 lb.*	*450 g.*	*1 lb.*
Chicken stock cube	*1*	*1*	*1*
Wine vinegar	*3 tbsp.*	*45 ml.*	*3 tbsp.*
Made mustard	*¼ tsp.*	*¼ tsp.*	*¼ tsp.*
Soy sauce	*1 tbsp.*	*15 ml.*	*1 tbsp.*
Light soft brown sugar	*1 oz.*	*25 g.*	*2 tbsp.*
Salt and pepper			
Cooked turkey	*1½ lb.*	*675 g.*	*1½ lb.*
Green pepper	*1 medium*	*1 medium*	*1 medium*
Onion	*1 small*	*1 small*	*1 small*
Cornflour	*½ oz.*	*15 g.*	*1 tbsp.*
Maraschino cherries	*2 oz.*	*50 g.*	*½ cup*

Drain the pineapple. Mix the syrup with the crumbled stock cube, vinegar, mustard, soy sauce and sugar and season with salt and pepper. Put into a casserole dish and mix well. Heat in the microwave oven for 5 minutes. Cut the turkey in cubes. Cut the green pepper in strips and slice the onion thinly. Stir turkey, pepper and onion into the casserole. Cover and microwave for 5 minutes. Mix the cornflour with a little water and stir into the mixture. Cover and microwave for 5 minutes until the sauce is clear and thick. Stir in the pineapple chunks and cherries and mix well. Cover and leave to stand for 2 minutes. Serve with rice or noodles.

REHEAT
15 minutes

PASTA AND RICE

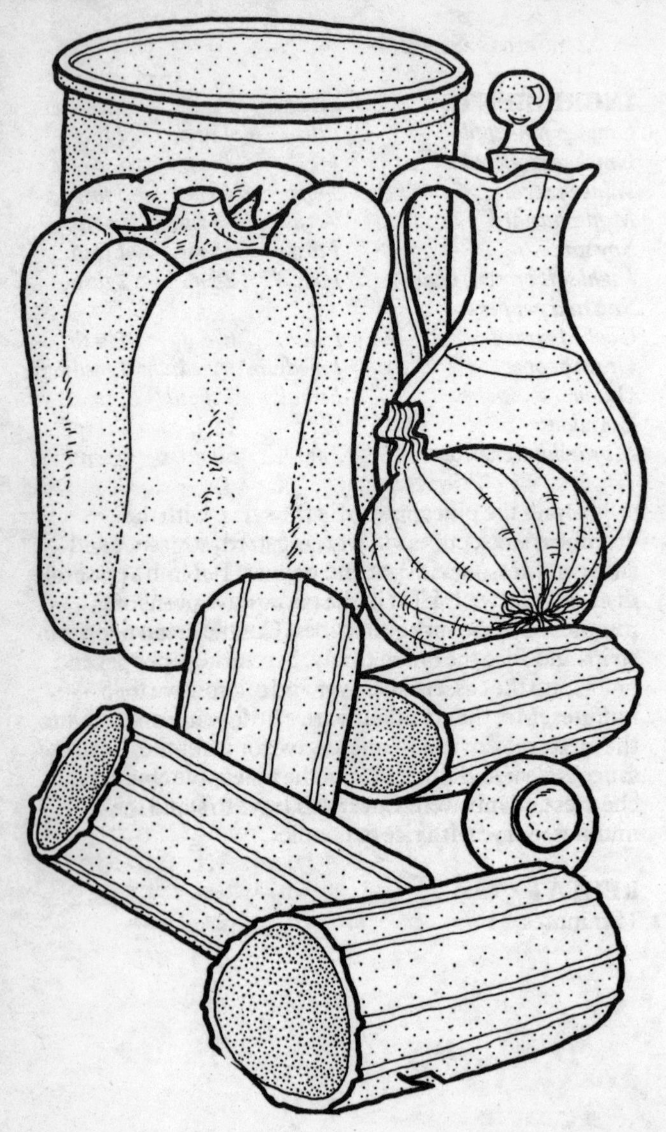

Cannelloni

✳ 2 months Serves 4

INGREDIENTS	Imperial	Metric	American
Cannelloni	*8 tubes*	*8 tubes*	*8 tubes*
Onion	*1 small*	*1 small*	*1 small*
Garlic clove	*1*	*1*	*1*
Green pepper	*1 small*	*1 small*	*1 small*
Oil	*2 tbsp.*	*30 ml.*	*2 tbsp.*
Chicken livers	*8 oz.*	*225 g.*	*8 oz.*
Button mushrooms	*8 oz.*	*225 g.*	*2 cups*
Canned tomatoes	*8 oz.*	*225 g.*	*8 oz.*
Boiling water	*1½ pt.*	*900 ml.*	*3¾ cups*
Cheese Sauce (see page 114 — White Sauce (variation)			
Grated Parmesan cheese	*1 tbsp.*	*1 tbsp.*	*1 tbsp.*

Put the cannelloni in a large pie dish and pour on the boiling water. Cook in the microwave oven for 10 minutes, moving the cannelloni once, and making sure that it is covered with water. Drain well and keep on one side. Chop the onion and crush the garlic clove. Cut the pepper in thin strips. Put the onion, garlic, pepper and oil into a shallow dish and microwave for 5 minutes, stirring twice. Add the chopped chicken livers and microwave for 3 minutes, stirring once. Add the sliced mushrooms and tomatoes with their liquid and microwave for 2 minutes. Fill the cannelloni tubes with this mixture and arrange in a shallow dish. Pour over the hot cheese sauce to cover the cannelloni completely. Sprinkle with cheese and microwave for 1 minute. Serve with a green salad.

SPECIAL INSTRUCTIONS
Freeze without cheese garnish. Sprinkle on before reheating.

REHEAT
10 minutes

Spaghetti Bolognese

✳ 2 months Serves 4

INGREDIENTS	Imperial	Metric	American
Short cut spaghetti	*8 oz.*	*225 g.*	*8 oz.*
Boiling water	*2 pt.*	*1.2 l.*	*5 cups*
Butter (or oil)	*1 oz.*	*25 g.*	*2 tbsp.*
Pinch of salt			
Raw minced beef	*1 lb.*	*450 g.*	*1 lb.*
Onion	*1 medium*	*1 medium*	*1 medium*
Green pepper	*1*	*1*	*1*
Garlic clove	*1*	*1*	*1*
Canned tomatoes	*1 lb.*	*450 g.*	*1 lb.*
Concentrated tomato purée	*2 tbsp.*	*2 tbsp.*	*2 tbsp.*
Beef stock cube	*1*	*1*	*1*
Red wine	*¼ pt.*	*150 ml.*	*⅔ cup*
Mixed herbs	*½ tsp.*	*½ tsp.*	*½ tsp.*
Salt and freshly ground black pepper			
Chopped parsley	*1 tbsp.*	*1 tbsp.*	*1 tbsp.*
Grated Parmesan cheese	*1 tbsp.*	*1 tbsp.*	*1 tbsp.*

Put the spaghetti into a large pie dish and pour on the boiling water. Cook in the microwave oven for 15 minutes, stirring twice. Add salt and leave to stand in water for 5 minutes. Drain well and rinse in boiling water. Stir a little oil or butter into the spaghetti so that it keeps separate, and keep warm. Put the mince into a shallow dish and add finely chopped onion, green pepper and crushed garlic. Cook in the microwave oven for 5 minutes. Stir in the tomatoes and their liquid, breaking them up with a fork. Add the purée, crumbled stock cube, wine and herbs, and season. Stir well and cover with clingfilm, making two small holes in the film. Cook in the microwave oven for 15 minutes, stirring twice. Leave to stand for 5 minutes and serve with spaghetti. Serve with Parmesan cheese and chopped parsley.

SPECIAL INSTRUCTIONS
Pack spaghetti and sauce separately for freezer. Arrange spaghetti in serving dish and place sauce on top to reheat.

REHEAT
10 minutes

Macaroni Cheese

∗ 2 months Serves 4

INGREDIENTS	Imperial	Metric	American
Short macaroni	*8 oz.*	*225 g.*	*8 oz.*
Boiling water	*2 pt.*	*1.2 l.*	*5 cups*
Salt	*1 tsp.*	*1 tsp.*	*1 tsp.*
Butter	*2 oz.*	*50 g.*	*4 tbsp.*
Onion	*1 small*	*1 small*	*1 small*
Lean bacon rashers	*2*	*2*	*2*
Plain flour	*1 oz.*	*25 g.*	*2 tbsp.*
Milk	*1 pt.*	*600 ml.*	*2½ cups*
Grated Cheddar cheese	*6 oz.*	*150 g.*	*1½ cups*
Salt and pepper			
Pinch of paprika			

Put the macaroni into a large bowl and add the hot water and salt. Cook in the microwave oven for 15 minutes, stirring twice. Put the butter into a bowl and heat in the microwave oven for 1 minute. Add the onion and bacon and cook for 4 minutes. Stir in the flour and add the milk gradually. Cook in the microwave oven for 5 minutes, stirring twice. Stir in the cheese and leave to stand for 2 minutes. Stir in the macaroni and season. Microwave for 4 minutes, stirring 4 times. Sprinkle with paprika before serving.

REHEAT
10 minutes

Spanish Rice

* 2 months Serves 4

INGREDIENTS	Imperial	Metric	American
Streaky bacon rashers	*3*	*3*	*3*
Onion	*1 large*	*1 large*	*1 large*
Green pepper	*1*	*1*	*1*
Red pepper	*1*	*1*	*1*
Garlic cloves	*2*	*2*	*2*
Oil	*2 tbsp.*	*30 ml.*	*2 tbsp.*
Button mushrooms	*4 oz.*	*100 g.*	*1 cup*
Long grain rice	*6 oz.*	*150 g.*	*¾ cup*
Chicken stock	*¾ pt.*	*450 ml.*	*2 cups*
Tomatoes	*3*	*3*	*3*
Black olives	*2 oz.*	*50 g.*	*⅓ cup*

Chop the bacon, onion and peppers, and crush the garlic cloves. Put into a bowl with the oil and cook in the microwave oven for 7 minutes, stirring twice. Add sliced mushrooms, rice and boiling stock. Stir well and cook in the microwave oven for 18 minutes until the rice has absorbed nearly all of the liquid. Stir two or three times during cooking. Stone the olives. Skin and chop the tomatoes. Stir the olives and tomatoes into the rice, and leave to stand for 3 minutes before serving.

SPECIAL INSTRUCTIONS
Freeze without olives. Stir in after reheating.

REHEAT
10 minutes

VEGETABLE DISHES

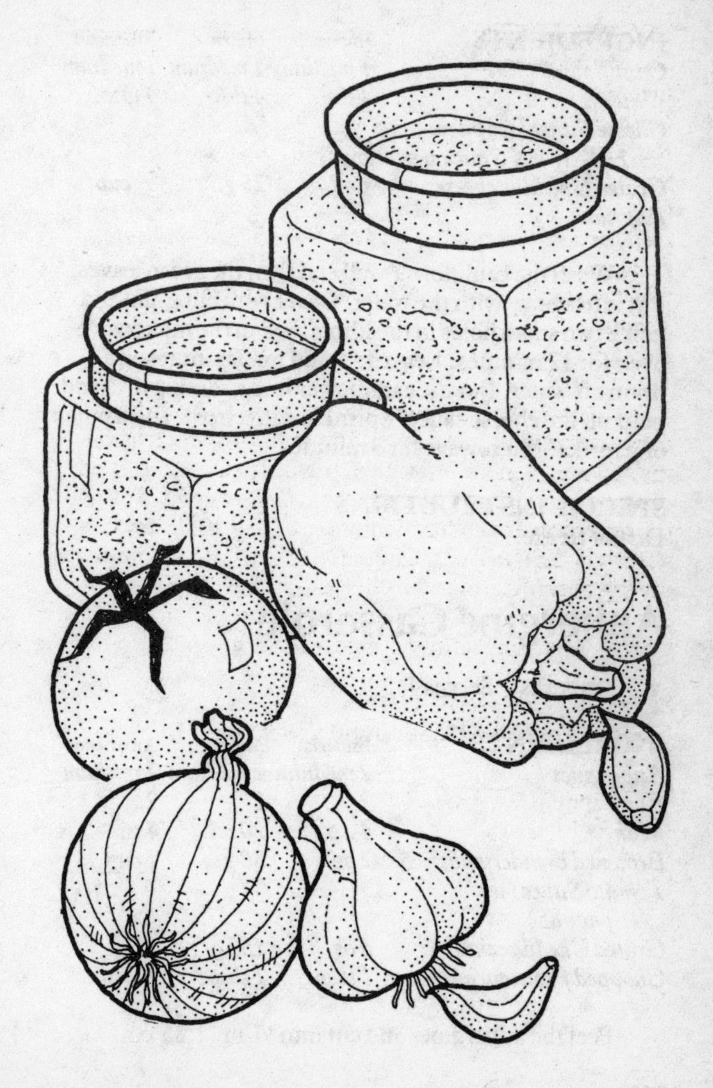

Cauliflower Cheese

Serves 4

INGREDIENTS	Imperial	Metric	American
Cauliflower	*1 medium*	*1 medium*	*1 medium*
Water	*4 tbsp.*	*4 tbsp.*	*4 tbsp.*
Cheese Sauce (see page 114–White Sauce variation			
Grated Cheddar cheese	*1 oz.*	*25 g.*	*1/4 cup*
Paprika			

Wash the cauliflower well and trim the green leaves. Put into a bowl with the water. Cover with clingfilm and make two small holes in the film. Cook in the microwave oven for 12 minutes. Leave to stand for 5 minutes and drain off water. Put the cauliflower into a serving dish and pour on the cheese sauce. Sprinkle with cheese and a pinch of paprika. Microwave for 3 minutes.

SPECIAL INSTRUCTIONS
Do not freeze.

Aubergine Casserole

* 2 months   Serves 4

INGREDIENTS	Imperial	Metric	American
Aubergines	*2 medium*	*2 medium*	*2 medium*
Eggs	*2*	*2*	*2*
Milk	*4 tsp.*	*20 ml.*	*4 tsp.*
Browned breadcrumbs	*2 oz.*	*50 g.*	*1 cup*
Tomato Sauce (see page 85)			
Grated Cheddar cheese	*6 oz.*	*150 g.*	*1 cup*
Chopped fresh marjoram	*1 tbsp.*	*1 tbsp.*	*1 tbsp.*

Peel the aubergines and cut into ½ in./1.25 cm.

slices. Beat the eggs with the milk in a bowl. Put the breadcrumbs on a flat plate. Dip the aubergine slices into the egg mixture and then into the breadcrumbs until well coated. Arrange layers of aubergine slices, tomato sauce and cheese in a greased rectangular dish and sprinkle with marjoram. Cover with clingfilm and cook in the microwave oven for 22 minutes. Leave to stand for 5 minutes before serving.

REHEAT
10 minutes

Creamed Beans and Corn

* 2 months Serves 4

INGREDIENTS	Imperial	Metric	American
Broad beans	*10 oz.*	*300 g.*	*10 oz.*
Sweetcorn kernels	*10 oz.*	*300 g.*	*10 oz.*
Green or red pepper	*½*	*½*	*½*
Salt and pepper			
Pinch of sugar			
Butter	*2 oz.*	*50 g.*	*¼ cup*
Single cream	*¼ pt.*	*150 ml.*	*⅔ cup*

If frozen vegetables are used for this dish, they should be thawed before use. Drained canned sweetcorn may be used, but should not be precooked with the beans. Put beans and corn into a casserole with 2 tablespoons water. Cover and cook in microwave oven for 12 minutes. Drain off any surplus liquid. Add very finely chopped pepper, salt and pepper and a pinch of sugar and stir well. Cut the butter into thin flakes and add to the vegetables with the cream. Stir well, cover and microwave for 3 minutes.

SPECIAL INSTRUCTIONS
Freeze without cream. Stir in after reheating.

REHEAT
10 minutes

Orange Glazed Carrots

* 2 months Serves 4

INGREDIENTS	Imperial	Metric	American
Carrots	*1 lb.*	*450 g.*	*1 lb.*
Dark soft brown sugar	*1½ oz.*	*40 g.*	*¼ cup*
Butter	*1½ oz.*	*40 g.*	*3 tbsp.*
Orange juice	*3 tbsp.*	*45 ml.*	*3 tbsp.*
Grated lemon peel	*1 tsp.*	*1 tsp.*	*1 tsp.*
Salt	*¼ tsp.*	*¼ tsp.*	*¼ tsp.*

Scrape or peel the carrots and cut them into thin slices. Put into a casserole with all the other ingredients and stir well. Cover and cook in the microwave oven for 13 minutes, stirring twice. These are particularly good served with ham.

REHEAT
10 minutes

Hot Spinach Salad

* Serves 4

INGREDIENTS	Imperial	Metric	American
Bacon rashers	6	6	6
Onion	*1 small*	*1 small*	*1 small*
Pepper			
Sugar	*½ oz.*	*15 g.*	*1 tbsp.*
Wine vinegar	*6 tbsp.*	*100 ml.*	*6 tbsp.*
Water	*6 tbsp.*	*100 ml.*	*6 tbsp.*
Fresh spinach	*1 lb.*	*450 g.*	*1 lb.*
Hard-boiled egg	*1*	*1*	*1*

Remove bacon rinds. Put bacon on a dish and cover with a piece of kitchen paper. Cook in microwave oven for 6 minutes until the bacon is crisp. Chop the bacon finely, and reserve any fat which has run out. Put the bacon fat into a bowl with finely chopped onion and microwave for 2½ minutes until the onion pieces are crisp. Stir in pepper, sugar, vinegar and water and microwave 2½ minutes. Meanwhile, wash the spinach and remove stems. Put the leaves into a serving bowl. Pour over hot dressing and toss with crumbled bacon and finely chopped egg.

SPECIAL INSTRUCTIONS
Do not freeze.

French Green Peas

* 2 months Serves 4

INGREDIENTS	Imperial	Metric	American
Butter	*1 oz.*	*25 g.*	*2 tbsp.*
Spring onions (scallions)	*4*	*4*	*4*
Crisp lettuce	*1*	*1*	*1*
Frozen peas	*10 oz.*	*350 g.*	*10 oz.*
Salt and pepper			

Put the butter into a vegetable serving dish. Chop the spring onions finely. Add to the butter and cook in microwave oven for 1 minute. Shred the lettuce finely and put into the dish with the peas, salt and pepper. Cover with clingfilm, and make two small holes in the top. Microwave for 2 minutes. Remove clingfilm and continue cooking for 2 minutes. Serve immediately.

REHEAT
5 minutes

Stuffed Mushrooms

* 2 months Serves 4

INGREDIENTS	Imperial	Metric	American
Large flat mushrooms	*8*	*8*	*8*
Butter	*2 oz.*	*50 g.*	*¼ cup*
Fresh breadcrumbs	*2 oz.*	*50 g.*	*1 cup*
Egg	*1*	*1*	*1*
Onion	*1 small*	*1 small*	*1 small*
Chopped fresh parsley	*1 tbsp.*	*1 tbsp.*	*1 tbsp.*
Salt and pepper			
Grated Parmesan cheese	*2 tbsp.*	*2 tbsp.*	*2 tbsp.*
Paprika			

Wipe the mushrooms clean and remove the stems. Chop the stems very finely. Put the butter into a bowl and heat in the microwave oven for 1 minute. Mix the butter with the breadcrumbs and beaten egg. Chop the onion finely and add to the breadcrumbs with the chopped mushroom stalks, parsley, salt and pepper. Spread the mixture on the inverted mushroom caps and place them on a piece of greaseproof paper on a flat dish. Sprinkle with cheese and a pinch of paprika. Microwave for 5 minutes and serve at once.

SPECIAL INSTRUCTIONS
Freeze without cheese and parsley. Sprinkle on before reheating.

REHEAT
5 minutes

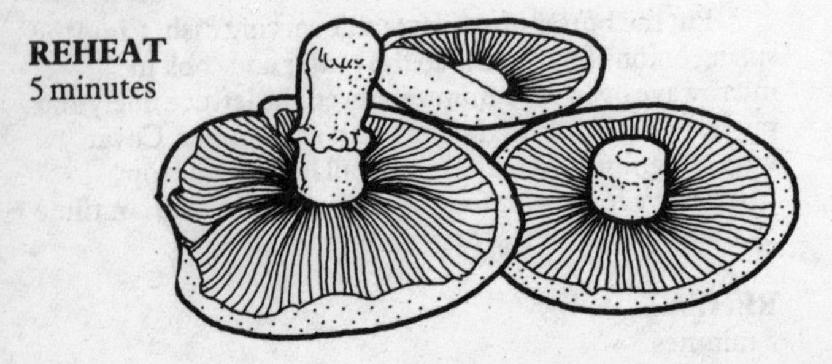

Ratatouille

∗ 2 months Serves 4

INGREDIENTS	Imperial	Metric	American
Butter	*1 oz.*	*25 g.*	*2 tbsp.*
Oil	*2 tbsp.*	*30 ml.*	*2 tbsp.*
Onions	*2 medium*	*2 medium*	*2 medium*
Garlic clove	*1–2*	*1–2*	*1–2*
Courgettes (zucchini)	*8 oz.*	*225 g.*	*8 oz.*
Aubergines	*12 oz.*	*350 g.*	*12 oz.*
Green pepper	*1*	*1*	*1*
Tomatoes	*8 oz.*	*225 g.*	*8 oz.*
Chopped fresh parsley	*2 tbsp.*	*2 tbsp.*	*2 tbsp.*
Salt and pepper			

Put the butter and oil in a casserole and heat in the microwave oven for 2 minutes. Slice the onions thinly and crush the garlic. Add to the fat and cook for 5 minutes. Do not peel the courgettes or aubergines but slice them thinly. Remove the seeds from the green pepper and cut the flesh in thin slices. Peel the tomatoes and chop coarsely. Stir the vegetables into the onions, stir well and cover with clingfilm. Make two small holes in the film. Cook in the microwave oven for 20 minutes, stirring twice during cooking. Uncover and cook for 7 minutes. Stir in parsley and season well. Serve hot or cold, with French bread.

SPECIAL INSTRUCTIONS
Freeze without parsley. Stir in after reheating.

THAW
At room temperature 3 hours
OR
REHEAT
8 minutes

Courgettes in Tomato Sauce

* 2 months Serves 4

INGREDIENTS	Imperial	Metric	American
Butter	*1 oz.*	*25 g.*	*2 tbsp.*
Oil	*2 tbsp.*	*30 ml.*	*2 tbsp.*
Courgettes (zucchini)	*1 lb.*	*450 g.*	*1 lb.*
Garlic cloves	*2*	*2*	*2*
Tomatoes	*4*	*4*	*4*
Mushrooms	*4 oz.*	*100 g.*	*1 cup*
Salt and pepper			
Chopped parsley	*1 tbsp.*	*1 tbsp.*	*1 tbsp.*

Wipe the courgettes clean but do not peel them. Cut across in ½ in./1.25 cm. slices. Put the butter and oil into a shallow dish and heat in the microwave oven for 1 minute. Stir in the courgettes and crushed garlic. Cover with clingfilm and microwave for 2 minutes. Skin the tomatoes, cut in half and discard seeds. Chop flesh roughly. Chop the mushrooms finely. Stir into the courgettes, cover and microwave again for 2 minutes. Season well, stir vegetables, cover and continue cooking for 2 minutes. Garnish with chopped parsley.

SPECIAL INSTRUCTIONS
Freeze without parsley. Sprinkle on after reheating.

REHEAT
10 minutes

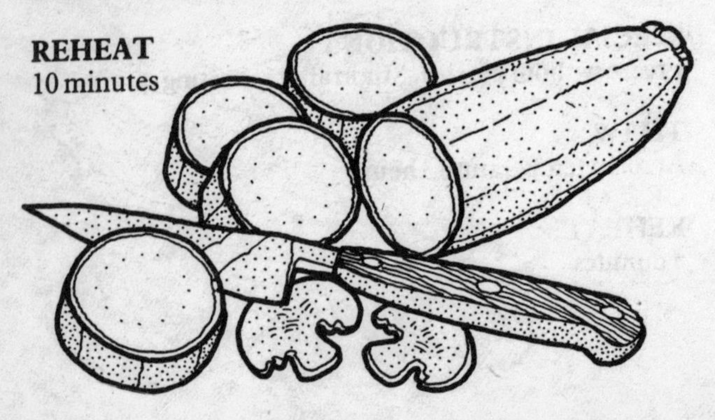

Red Cabbage Casserole

✻ 2 months Serves 4–6

INGREDIENTS	Imperial	Metric	American
Red cabbage	*2 lb.*	*900 g.*	*2 lb.*
Water	*4 tbsp.*	*60 ml.*	*4 tbsp.*
Eating apple	*1*	*1*	*1*
Salt and freshly ground black pepper			
Onion	*1 small*	*1 small*	*1 small*
Dark soft brown sugar	*1½ oz.*	*40 g.*	*¼ cup*
Caraway seeds	*½ tsp.*	*½ tsp.*	*½ tsp.*
Vinegar	*6 tbsp.*	*90 ml.*	*6 tbsp.*
Ground mixed spice	*½ tsp.*	*½ tsp.*	*½ tsp.*

Shred the cabbage finely and put into a covered casserole with the water. Cook in the microwave oven for 6 minutes. Peel and core the apple and chop finely. Add to the cabbage with the salt and pepper and stir well. Add grated onion, sugar and caraway seeds. Mix the spice with a little of the vinegar, and then stir into the cabbage with the remaining vinegar. Stir very thoroughly. Cover and continue to microwave for 8 minutes, stirring twice. If there is any cabbage left after serving hot, it makes a good salad when cold.

REHEAT
10 minutes

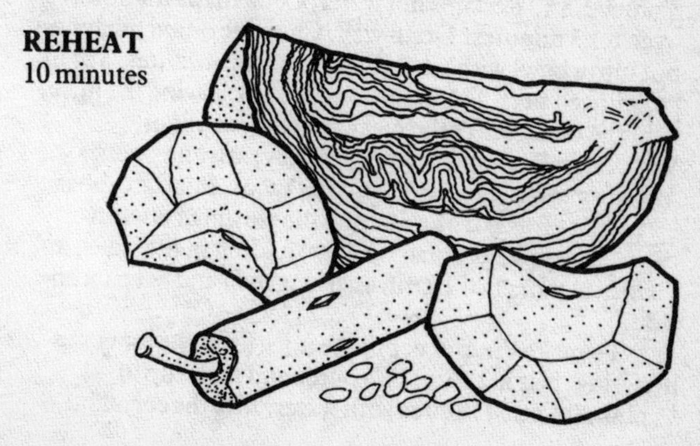

Stuffed Cabbage in Tomato Sauce

✻ 2 months Serves 4–6

INGREDIENTS	Imperial	Metric	American
Cabbage leaves	*8 large*	*8 large*	*8 large*
Onion	*1 medium*	*1 medium*	*1 medium*
Oil	*1 tbsp.*	*15 ml.*	*1 tbsp.*
Raw minced beef	*1 lb.*	*450 g.*	*1 lb.*
Canned tomatoes	*14 oz.*	*400 g.*	*14 oz.*
Cornflour	*2 tsp.*	*2 tsp.*	*2 tsp.*
Worcestershire sauce	*1 tbsp.*	*1 tbsp.*	*1 tbsp.*
Dried mixed herbs	*¼ tsp.*	*¼ tsp.*	*¼ tsp.*
Chopped fresh parsley	*1 tbsp.*	*1 tbsp.*	*1 tbsp.*
Salt and pepper			
Sauce			
Tomato purée	*1 tbsp.*	*1 tbsp.*	*1 tbsp.*
Cornflour	*2 tsp.*	*2 tsp.*	*2 tsp.*
Worcestershire sauce	*1 tsp.*	*1 tsp.*	*1 tsp.*
Sugar	*½ tsp.*	*½ tsp.*	*½ tsp.*
Salt and pepper			

Put the cabbage leaves into a large bowl. Cover with 3 pints/1.8 l./7½ cups hot water. Cook in the microwave oven for 3 minutes. Drain well. Chop the onion finely and put into a bowl with oil. Microwave for 2 minutes. Stir in the minced beef. Drain the tomatoes, reserving the juice. Add the tomatoes to the meat with the cornflour, Worcestershire sauce, herbs, parsley, salt and pepper. Microwave for 6 minutes, stirring twice. Put the cabbage leaves flat on a board and divide the stuffing between them. Roll up the cabbage leaves, folding in the sides, to form neat parcels. Place in a serving dish and keep on one side.

To make the sauce, put the juice from the tomatoes into a jug. Stir in the tomato purée and make up to ½ pint/300 ml./1¼ cups with water. Mix the cornflour with a little of this liquid and add with the Worcestershire sauce, sugar, salt and pepper. Cook in the microwave oven for 3 minutes, stirring twice. Pour over the stuffed cabbage leaves and microwave for 2 minutes.

REHEAT
15 minutes

Stuffed Tomatoes

* 1 month Serves 4

INGREDIENTS	Imperial	Metric	American
Tomatoes	*4 large*	*4 large*	*4 large*
Cooked ham	*4 oz.*	*100 g.*	*½ cup*
Onion	*1 small*	*1 small*	*1 small*
Fresh breadcrumbs	*1 oz.*	*25 g.*	*½ cup*
Button mushrooms	*2 oz.*	*50 g.*	*½ cup*
Grated Parmesan cheese	*1 tbsp.*	*1 tbsp.*	*1 tbsp.*
Chopped fresh parsley	*1 tbsp.*	*1 tbsp.*	*1 tbsp.*

Cut the tops from the tomatoes about 1½ ins./3.75 cm. down from the stalk. Using a small spoon, scoop out the flesh in the centre. Put this through a sieve to get rid of the pips. Chop the ham, onion and mushrooms very finely. Mix with the tomato juice and breadcrumbs. Cook in microwave oven for 2 minutes. Spoon the mixture into the tomatoes and stand them in a shallow serving dish. Microwave for 1 minute. Sprinkle with cheese, and then with parsley and serve at once.

SPECIAL INSTRUCTIONS
Freeze without cheese and parsley. Garnish after reheating.

REHEAT
5 minutes

Stuffed Baked Potatoes

* 1 month Serves 4

INGREDIENTS	Imperial	Metric	American
Potatoes	*4 large (6 oz. each)*	*4 large (150 g. each)*	*4 large (6 oz. each)*
Various fillings (see below)			

Scrub the potatoes well and prick the skins all over with a fork. Cook in the microwave oven for 8 minutes. Turn the potatoes and continue cooking for 6 minutes. Take out of the oven and leave to stand for 5 minutes. Cut the top from each potato and scoop out the potato flesh into a bowl, leaving a 'wall' of flesh and potato skin. Mix the potato with chosen filling and refill the potatoes. Sprinkle with 1 oz./25 g./¼ cup grated Cheddar cheese and microwave for 3 minutes.

FILLINGS

Minced Beef While the potatoes are standing, microwave 8 oz./225 g./8 oz. raw minced beef and 1 small onion, chopped finely, for 4 minutes. Mix with the potato with 1 tablespoon tomato ketchup, salt and pepper.

Smoked Fish Cut the corner of a boil-in-the-bag containing 6 oz./150 g./6 oz. smoked haddock. Put the bag on a plate and cook in microwave oven for 5 minutes. Remove any skin from the fish and break the flesh into flakes. Mix fish with the potato, 2 oz./50 g./¼ cup butter, salt and pepper.

Ham and Cheese Mix 4 oz./100 g./1 cup finely chopped cooked ham with 2 oz./50 g./½ cup grated Cheddar cheese, 1 oz./25 g./2 tablespoons butter, 2 teaspoons Worcestershire sauce, salt and pepper.

REHEAT

5 minutes for each potato

SAUCES

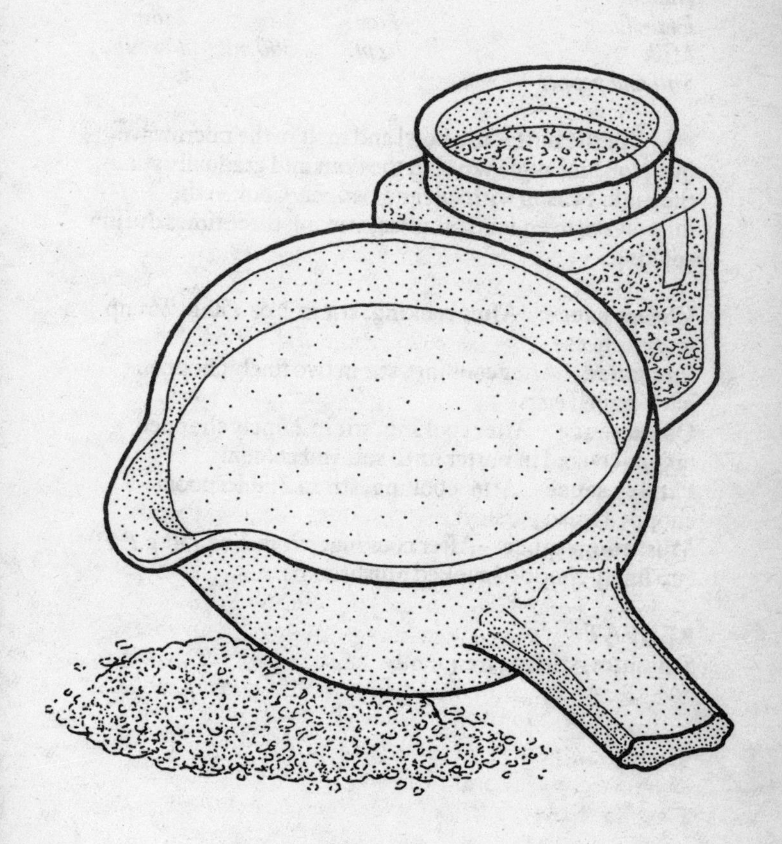

White Sauce

* 2 months

INGREDIENTS	Imperial	Metric	American
Butter	*1 oz.*	*25 g.*	*2 tbsp.*
Plain flour	*1 oz.*	*25 g.*	*2 tbsp.*
Milk	*½ pt.*	*300 ml.*	*1¼ cups*
Salt and pepper			

Put the butter in a bowl and melt in the microwave oven for 1 minute. Work in the flour and gradually stir in the milk. Season with salt and pepper. Cook in the microwave oven for 6 minutes, stirring three times during cooking.

Cheese sauce After cooking, stir in 2 oz./50 g./⅓ cup grated cheese.
Egg sauce After cooking, stir in two finely chopped hard-boiled eggs.
Onion sauce After cooking, stir in 2 finely chopped onions cooked in butter until soft and golden.
Parsley sauce After cooking, stir in 2 tablespoons chopped fresh parsley.
Mushroom sauce After cooking, stir in 2 oz./50 g./½ cup finely chopped cooked mushrooms.

REHEAT
5 minutes, stirring frequently

Bread Sauce

* 2 months

INGREDIENTS	Imperial	Metric	American
Onion	*1 small*	*1 small*	*1 small*
Cloves	6	6	6
Milk	*½ pt.*	*300 ml.*	*1¼ cups*
Fresh white breadcrumbs	*3 oz.*	*75 g.*	*1½ cups*
Butter	*1 oz.*	*25 g.*	*2 tbsp.*
Salt and pepper			
Single cream	*2 tbsp.*	*2 tbsp.*	*2 tbsp.*

Peel the onion and keep it whole. Stick the cloves into the onion. Put into a bowl with the milk and cook in the microwave oven for 4 minutes. Remove and discard the onion. Stir the breadcrumbs and butter into the milk and cook in the microwave for 2 minutes. Season with salt and pepper and stir in the cream. Microwave for 30 seconds and serve hot with poultry or game.

SPECIAL INSTRUCTIONS
Freeze without cream. Stir in after reheating.

REHEAT
5 minutes, stirring frequently

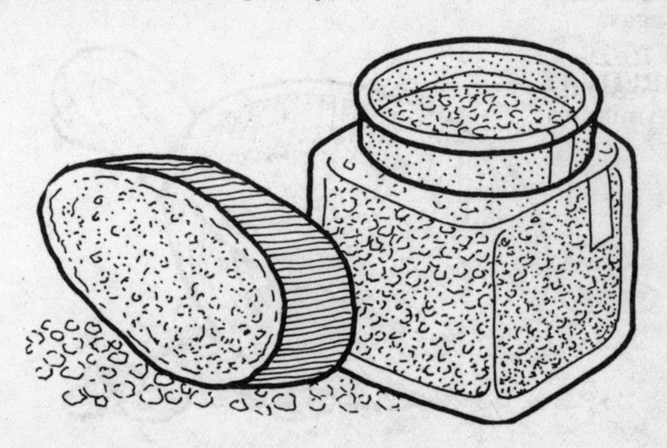

Curry Sauce

✱ 2 months

INGREDIENTS	Imperial	Metric	American
Onion	*1 medium*	*1 medium*	*1 medium*
Oil	*2 tbsp.*	*2 tbsp.*	*2 tbsp.*
Plain flour	*1 oz.*	*25 g.*	*2 tbsp.*
Curry powder	*2–3 tbsp.*	*2–3 tbsp.*	*2–3 tbsp.*
Curry paste	*1 tsp.*	*1 tsp.*	*1 tsp.*
Beef or chicken stock	*¾ pt.*	*450 ml.*	*2 cups*
Eating apple	*1*	*1*	*1*
Sultanas (white raisins)	*2 oz.*	*50 g.*	*⅓ cup*
Lemon juice	*2 tsp.*	*2 tsp.*	*2 tsp.*
Salt and pepper			
Caster sugar	*A pinch*	*A pinch*	*A pinch*

Chop the onion finely. Put the oil in a bowl and heat in the microwave oven for 30 seconds. Add the onion and continue cooking for 4 minutes, stirring once during cooking. Stir in the flour and curry powder and paste, mixing well, and then the stock. Peel and chop the apple and add to the bowl with the remaining ingredients. Cook in the microwave oven for 8 minutes, stirring twice during cooking. Serve with meat, poultry, vegetables, seafood or eggs.

REHEAT
5 minutes

Tomato Sauce

* 2 months

INGREDIENTS	Imperial	Metric	American
Onion	*1 medium*	*1 medium*	*1 medium*
Garlic clove	*1*	*1*	*1*
Olive oil	*1 tbsp.*	*15 ml.*	*1 tbsp.*
Ripe tomatoes	*1 lb.*	*450 g.*	*1 lb.*
Salt	*1 tsp.*	*1 tsp.*	*1 tsp.*
Sugar	*1 tsp.*	*1 tsp.*	*1 tsp.*
Paprika	*1 tsp.*	*1 tsp.*	*1 tsp.*
Vinegar	*1 tbsp.*	*1 tbsp.*	*1 tbsp.*
Bay leaf	*1*	*1*	*1*
Pepper			

Chop the onion finely and crush the garlic. Put into a bowl with the oil and cook in the microwave oven for 4 minutes. Stir twice while cooking. Skin the tomatoes and take out and discard pips. Cut the flesh in small pieces. Add all the ingredients to the bowl and continue cooking for 7 minutes, stirring twice. Remove the bay leaf and discard. For a smooth sauce, put through a sieve or blend in a liquidiser; for use with pasta, the sauce need not be smooth. After sieving or blending, reheat in the microwave for 2 minutes. Serve with pasta, meat, fish or vegetables.

REHEAT
5 minutes

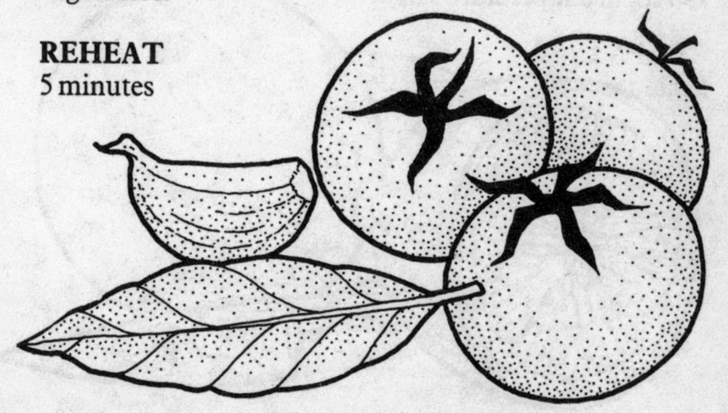

Cumberland Sauce

∗ 2 months

INGREDIENTS	Imperial	Metric	American
Orange	*1*	*1*	*1*
Lemon	*1*	*1*	*1*
Shallot	*1*	*1*	*1*
Redcurrant jelly	*8 oz.*	*225 g.*	*1 cup*
Port	*¼ pt.*	*150 ml.*	*⅔ cup*
Made mustard	*½ tsp.*	*½ tsp.*	*½ tsp.*
Ground ginger	*½ tsp.*	*½ tsp.*	*½ tsp.*
Cayenne pepper			

Peel the orange and lemon very thinly, making sure that no white pith is attached. Cut the peel into needle-thin shreds. Chop the shallot very finely and pour on a little boiling water. Leave to stand for 1 minute and drain well. Put the fruit peel and shallot into a bowl. Squeeze the juice from the orange and lemon and strain into the bowl. Add the redcurrant jelly. Heat in the microwave oven for 4 minutes. Stir in the port, mustard, ginger and pinch of Cayenne pepper. Heat in the microwave for 1 minute. Cool and serve with ham or pork.

THAW
At room temperature 3 hours

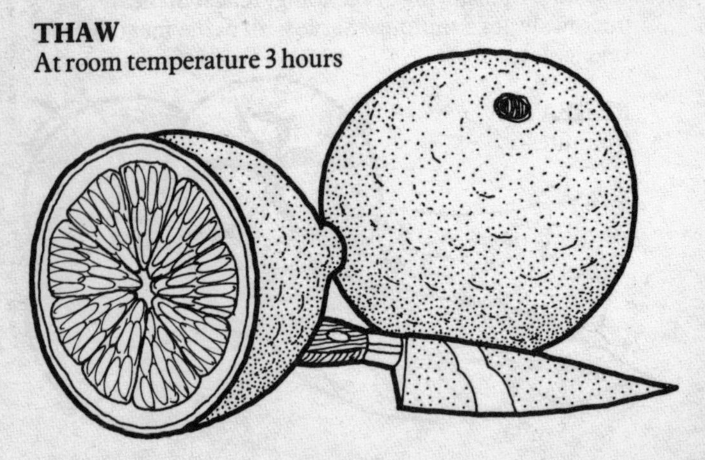

Barbecue Sauce

* 2 months

INGREDIENTS	Imperial	Metric	American
Onion	*1 medium*	*1 medium*	*1 medium*
Butter	*1 oz.*	*25 g.*	*2 tbsp.*
Plain flour	*½ oz.*	*15 g.*	*1 tbsp.*
Made mustard	*2 tsp.*	*2 tsp.*	*2 tsp.*
Worcestershire sauce	*1 tbsp.*	*1 tbsp.*	*1 tbsp.*
Tabasco sauce	*1 tsp.*	*1 tsp.*	*1 tsp.*
Dark soft brown sugar	*½ oz.*	*15 g.*	*1 tbsp.*
Salt	*1 tsp.*	*1 tsp.*	*1 tsp.*
Vinegar	*1 tbsp.*	*1 tbsp.*	*1 tbsp.*
Tomato juice	*½ pt.*	*300 ml.*	*1¼ cups*

Chop the onion finely. Put into a bowl with the butter and cook in the microwave oven for 4 minutes. Stir in the flour and then all the remaining ingredients. Cook in the microwave oven for 8 minutes, stirring twice during cooking. Serve hot with chicken, steak, chops, sausages or burgers.

REHEAT
5 minutes

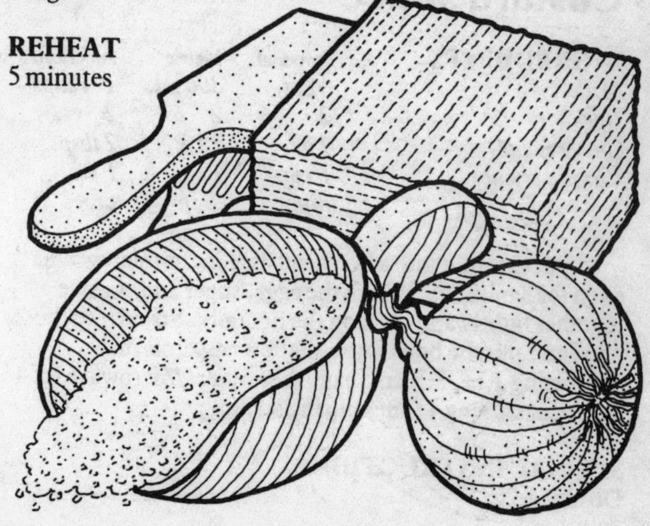

Apple Sauce

* 2 months

INGREDIENTS	Imperial	Metric	American
Cooking apples	*1 lb.*	*450 g.*	*1 lb.*
Water	*2 tbsp.*	*30 ml.*	*2 tbsp.*
Sugar	*2 oz.*	*50 g.*	*¼ cup*
Butter	*1 oz.*	*25 g.*	*2 tbsp.*

Peel and core the apples and cut them into thin slices. Put into a bowl with the other ingredients. Cook in the microwave oven for 3 minutes, stirring twice during cooking. Sieve or blend in a liquidiser until smooth. Reheat in microwave oven for 30 seconds and serve hot with pork or duck.

REHEAT
5 minutes

Custard Sauce

INGREDIENTS	Imperial	Metric	American
Milk	*½ pt.*	*300 ml.*	*1¼ cups*
Eggs	*2*	*2*	*2*
Caster sugar	*1 oz.*	*25 g.*	*2 tbsp.*
Vanilla essence	*Few drops*	*Few drops*	*Few drops*

Put the milk into a bowl and heat in the microwave oven for 3 minutes. Whisk the eggs, sugar and essence together lightly and pour on the hot milk. Strain into the bowl and put the bowl into a shallow casserole dish containing 1 in./2.5 cm. hand-hot water. Microwave for 4 minutes, stirring 4 times during cooking.

SPECIAL INSTRUCTIONS
Do not freeze.

Chocolate Sauce

✳ 2 months

INGREDIENTS	Imperial	Metric	American
Water	*¼ pt.*	*150 ml.*	*⅔ cup*
Caster sugar	*4 oz.*	*100 g.*	*½ cup*
Cocoa powder	*2 oz.*	*50 g.*	*4 tbsp.*

Put the water into a jug and heat in the microwave oven for 3 minutes. Stir in the sugar until dissolved. Microwave for 2 minutes. Whisk in the cocoa powder and microwave for 1 minute. As the sauce cools and thickens, stir occasionally. Serve hot or cold over ices and puddings.

THAW
At room temperature 3 hours
OR
REHEAT
5 minutes

Lemon Butter

✳ 2 months

INGREDIENTS	Imperial	Metric	American
Butter	*4 oz.*	*100 g.*	*½ cup*
Lemon juice	*1 tbsp.*	*15 ml.*	*1 tbsp.*
Pepper			

Cut the butter into small pieces and put in a bowl with the lemon juice and pepper. Heat in the microwave for 1½ minutes. Stir well and serve with fish or vegetables.

REHEAT
2 minutes

Butterscotch Sauce

* 2 months

INGREDIENTS	Imperial	Metric	American
Single cream	*¼ pt.*	*150 ml.*	*⅔ cup*
Dark soft brown sugar	*8 oz.*	*225 g.*	*1⅓ cups*
Butter	*1½ oz.*	*40 g.*	*3 tbsp.*
Vanilla essence	*Few drops*	*Few drops*	*Few drops*

Stir the cream, sugar and butter together in a bowl. Heat in the microwave oven for 4 minutes, stirring twice during cooking. Stir in vanilla essence. Serve with ices or puddings.

REHEAT
5 minutes

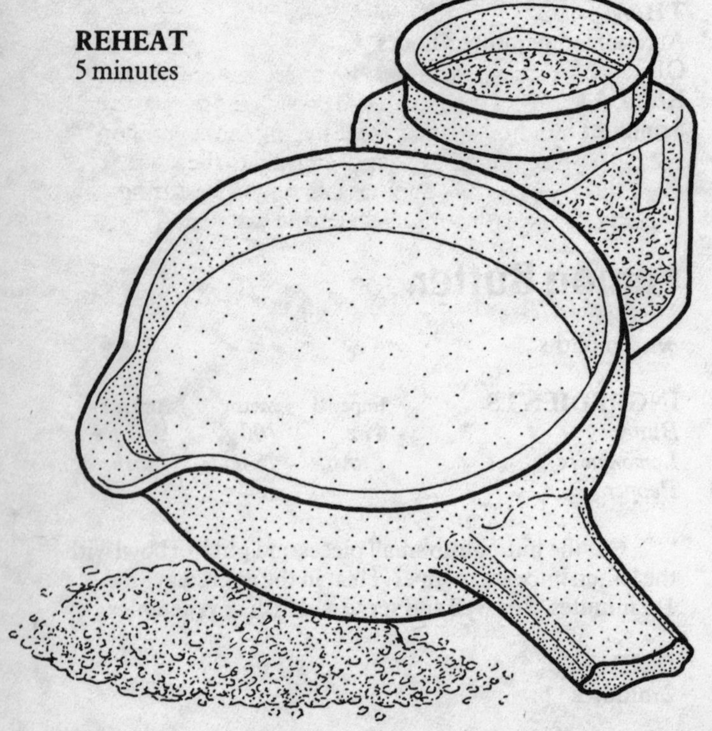

Sweet and Sour Sauce

*. 2 months

INGREDIENTS	Imperial	Metric	American
Sugar	*1½ oz.*	*40 g.*	*3 tbsp.*
Cornflour	*1 tbsp.*	*1 tbsp.*	*1 tbsp.*
Soy sauce	*2 tsp.*	*2 tsp.*	*2 tsp.*
Vinegar	*2 tbsp.*	*30 ml.*	*2 tbsp.*
Tomato purée	*2 tsp.*	*2 tsp.*	*2 tsp.*
Salt			
Chicken stock	*½ pt.*	*300 ml.*	*1¼ cups*
Canned pineapple, drained	*4 oz.*	*100 g.*	*4 oz.*
Onion	*1 small*	*1 small*	*1 small*
Green pepper	*½*	*½*	*½*

Mix the sugar, cornflour, soy sauce, vinegar, tomato purée, salt and chicken stock and cook in the microwave oven for 4 minutes, stirring twice during cooking. Chop the pineapple, onion and pepper and add to the sauce. Continue cooking for 3 minutes, stirring twice during cooking. Serve with pork, chicken and seafood.

REHEAT
5 minutes, stirring frequently

PUDDINGS

Baked Apples

* 2 months Serves 4

INGREDIENTS	Imperial	Metric	American
Cooking apples	*4 large*	*4 large*	*4 large*
Maple syrup	*¼ pt.*	*150 ml.*	*⅔ cup*
Butter	*1 oz.*	*25 g.*	*2 tbsp.*

Core the apples without peeling them, and score round the skin with a sharp knife. Put the apples in a shallow dish and pour syrup over them. Put a piece of butter in the centre of each apple. Cover with clingfilm, making two small holes in the film. Cook for 8 minutes in the microwave oven. Serve hot with cream or custard.

Brown Sugar Apples

Prepare the apples in the same way, but substitute 2 oz./50 g./4 tablespoons dark soft brown sugar and 4 tablespoons water for the maple syrup.

REHEAT
5 minutes

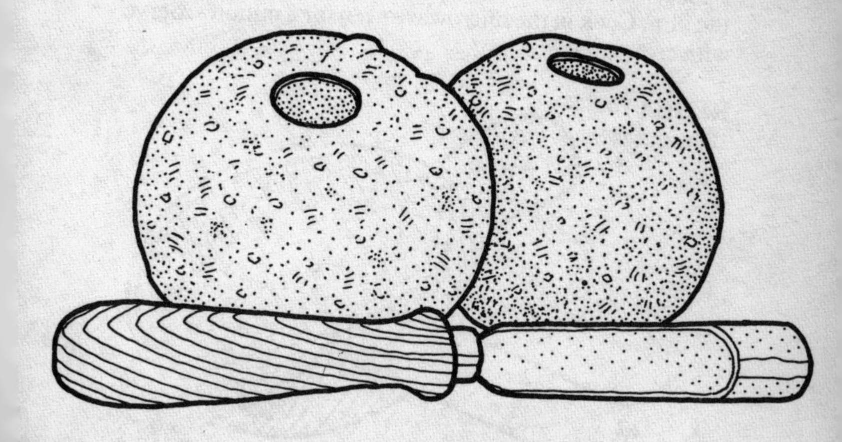

Apple Betty

* 2 months Serves 6

INGREDIENTS	Imperial	Metric	American
Eating apples	*6*	*6*	*6*
Light soft brown sugar	*3 oz.*	*75 g.*	*½ cup*
Soft white breadcrumbs	*1 oz.*	*25 g.*	*½ cup*
Lemon	*1*	*1*	*1*
Ground ginger	*½ tsp.*	*½ tsp.*	*½ tsp.*
Water	*2 tbsp.*	*2 tbsp.*	*2 tbsp.*
Dry breadcrumbs	*¼ oz.*	*7 g.*	*2 tbsp.*
Butter	*1 oz.*	*25 g.*	*2 tbsp.*

Peel and core the apples and slice them thinly. Put half the apple slices in the base of a soufflé dish. Mix 2 oz./50 g./4 tablespoons brown sugar with the soft breadcrumbs and sprinkle on to the apples. Cover with the remaining apple slices. Grate the lemon rind and squeeze out the juice. Mix the rind and juice with the ginger and water and pour evenly over the fruit. Mix the remaining sugar with the dry breadcrumbs and sprinkle over the fruit. Cut the butter into thin flakes and dot over the surface. Cover with clingfilm, making two small holes in the film. Cook in the microwave oven for 8 minutes. Serve with cream or ice cream.

REHEAT
10 minutes

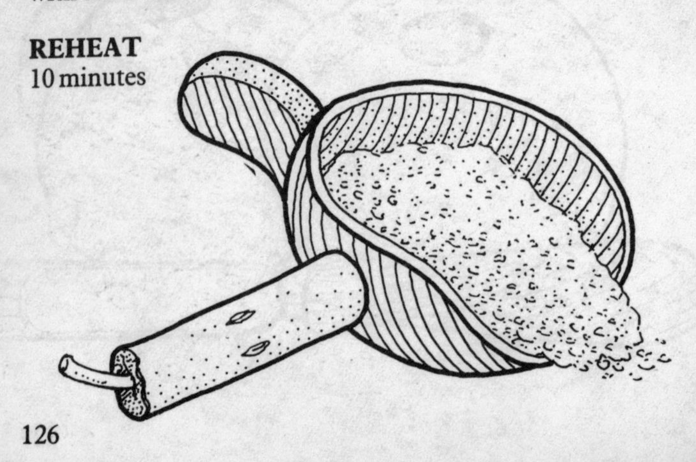

Apple and Apricot Compôte

* 2 months Serves 4

INGREDIENTS	Imperial	Metric	American
Eating apples	*2*	*2*	*2*
Sugar	*1½ oz.*	*40 g.*	*3 tbsp.*
Canned apricot halves	*1 lb.*	*450 g.*	*1 lb.*
Chopped walnuts	*2 oz.*	*50 g.*	*½ cup*
Ground cinnamon	*¼ tsp.*	*¼ tsp.*	*¼ tsp.*
Pinch of ground nutmeg			
Pinch of ground cloves			

Peel and core the apples and cut into thin slices. Put into a casserole dish and sprinkle with sugar. Cover and cook in the microwave oven for 3 minutes. Drain the apricots and stir the fruit into the apples. Add 4 tablespoons syrup from the can. Stir in the nuts and spices. Microwave uncovered for 4 minutes. Serve warm with cream. Canned peach slices, pears or pineapple may be used instead of apricots.

REHEAT
10 minutes

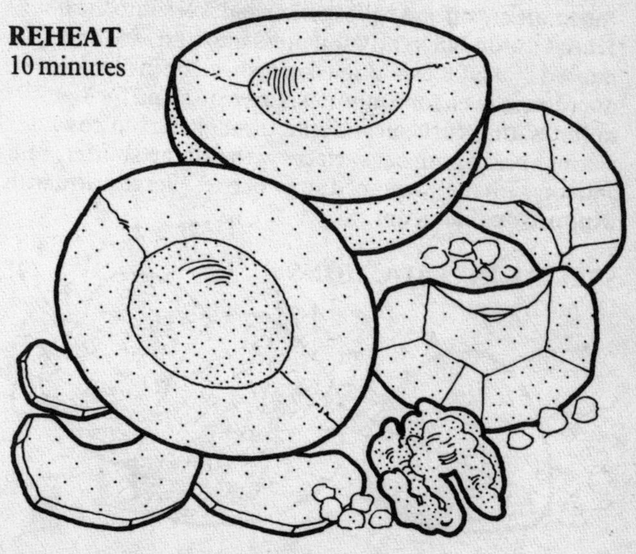

Strawberry Shortcake

Serves 8

INGREDIENTS	Imperial	Metric	American
Strawberries	*2 lb.*	*900 g.*	*2 lb.*
Caster sugar	*6 oz.*	*150 g.*	*¾ cup*
Plain flour	*8 oz.*	*225 g.*	*2 cups*
Baking powder	*3 tsp.*	*3 tsp.*	*3 tsp.*
Sugar	*1½ oz.*	*40 g.*	*3 tbsp.*
Butter or margarine	*4 oz.*	*100 g.*	*½ cup*
Single cream	*5 tbsp.*	*75 ml.*	*5 tbsp.*
Egg	*1*	*1*	*1*
Softened butter	*2 oz.*	*50 g.*	*4 tbsp.*
Double cream	*¼ pt.*	*150 ml.*	*⅔ cup*

Wash the strawberries and slice them thickly. Place in a bowl with the caster sugar, stir well and leave in the refrigerator for 1 hour. Sift the flour and baking powder together and stir in the sugar. Rub in the butter or margarine until the mixture is like fine breadcrumbs. Beat the single cream and egg together and work into the flour. Knead the dough lightly and press into a greased and floured 8 ins./20 cm. china flan dish. Cook in the microwave oven for 6 minutes. Leave to stand for 4 minutes, then turn out and split through the centre while warm. Spread both cut surfaces with softened butter. Fill and top with the sweetened strawberries. Serve warm with whipped double cream.

SPECIAL INSTRUCTIONS
Do not freeze.

Spiced Pears

* 2 months Serves 4

INGREDIENTS

	Imperial	Metric	American
Pears	*4*	*4*	*4*
Red wine	*½ pt.*	*300 ml.*	*1¼ cups*
Water	*½ pt.*	*300 ml.*	*1¼ cups*
Sugar	*2 oz.*	*50 g.*	*4 tbsp.*
Cinnamon stick	*1 × 2 ins.*	*1 × 5 cm.*	*1 × 2 ins.*
Cloves	*4*	*4*	*4*
Pinch of ground nutmeg			
Piece of lemon peel			
Lemon juice	*½ tsp.*	*½ tsp.*	*½ tsp.*
Flaked almonds	*2 tbsp.*	*2 tbsp.*	*2 tbsp.*

The pears should be ripe but firm, and even-sized. Peel them carefully and leave the fruit whole with the stalks on. Put the wine, water, sugar, spices, lemon peel and juice into a pie dish and cook in the microwave oven for 5 minutes. Stand the pears in the liquid with stalks uppermost. Microwave for 5 minutes. Leave to stand for 5 minutes, spooning the liquid over the pears a few times. Remove the cinnamon stick, cloves and lemon peel. Sprinkle each pear with almonds and serve with cream.

REHEAT
10 minutes

Caramel Oranges

∗ 2 months Serves 4

INGREDIENTS	Imperial	Metric	American
Oranges	*4*	*4*	*4*
Caster sugar	*6 oz.*	*150 g.*	*¾ cup*
Water	*7 tbsp.*	*100 ml.*	*7 tbsp.*
Orange liqueur	*1 tbsp.*	*15 ml.*	*1 tbsp.*

Peel the oranges carefully, making sure that all the white pith is removed. Cut across in slices and arrange in a serving dish. Sprinkle with the orange liqueur. Put the sugar and water into a basin and stir well. Cook in the microwave oven for 12 minutes until dark golden. Pour over the oranges and chill before serving.

THAW
At room temperature 3 hours

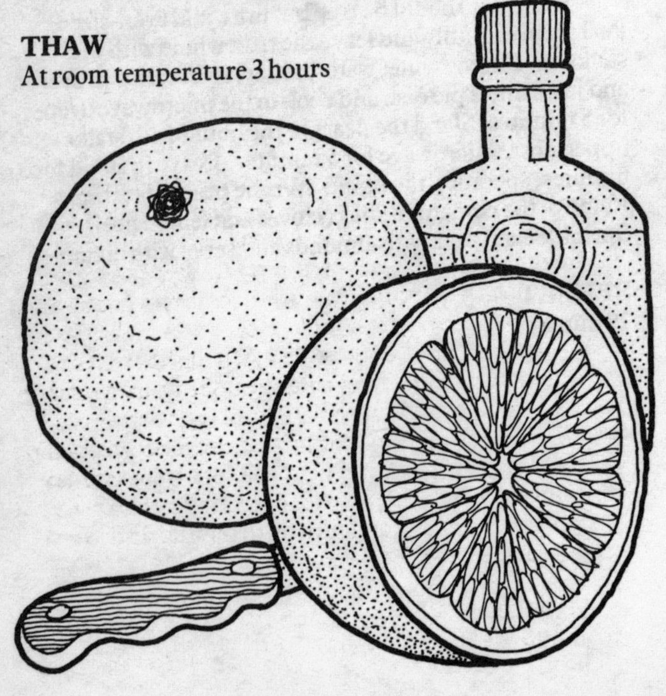

Chocolate Walnut Upside-Down Pudding

* 2 months Serves 8–10

INGREDIENTS	Imperial	Metric	American
Butter or margarine	*4 oz.*	*100 g.*	*½ cup*
Dark soft brown sugar	*3 oz.*	*75 g.*	*½ cup*
Walnut halves	*30*	*30*	*30*
Desiccated coconut	*3 oz.*	*75 g.*	*¾ cup*
Milk	*2 tbsp.*	*30 ml.*	*2 tbsp.*
Plain chocolate	*3 oz.*	*75 g.*	*3 squares*
Self-raising flour	*4 oz.*	*100 g.*	*1 cup*
Granulated sugar	*5½ oz.*	*140 g.*	*⅔ cup*
Baking powder	*¼ tsp.*	*¼ tsp.*	*¼ tsp.*
Bicarbonate of soda	*¼ tsp.*	*¼ tsp.*	*¼ tsp.*
Salt	*¼ tsp.*	*¼ tsp.*	*¼ tsp.*
Vanilla essence	*½ tsp.*	*½ tsp.*	*½ tsp.*
Sour milk	*¼ pt.*	*150 ml.*	*⅔ cup*
Egg	*1*	*1*	*1*

Grease an 8 ins./20 cm. square baking dish and line the base with greaseproof paper. Put half the butter in the dish and heat in the microwave oven for 1 minute. Stir in the brown sugar and spread the mixture evenly over the base of the dish. Arrange walnut halves in this mixture and sprinkle with coconut and milk. Heat the chocolate in a bowl for 1½ minutes until melted. Sift together the dry ingredients and add the remaining butter, vanilla essence and half the sour milk. Beat hard until the mixture is smooth and creamy. Add the melted chocolate, remaining milk and egg and beat until light and soft. Pour into the dish and bake in the microwave oven for 9 minutes. Leave to stand for 5 minutes and turn on to serving dish. Serve with cream.

REHEAT
10 minutes

Baked Orange Cheesecake

∗ 2 months Serves 6

INGREDIENTS	Imperial	Metric	American
Butter or margarine	*2 oz.*	*50 g.*	*4 tbsp.*
Digestive biscuits (Graham crackers)	*12*	*12*	*12*
Caster sugar	*4 oz.*	*100 g.*	*½ cup*
Full fat soft cream cheese	*8 oz.*	*225 g.*	*8 oz.*
Eggs	*2*	*2*	*2*
Concentrated orange juice	*2 tbsp.*	*30 ml.*	*2 tbsp.*
Lemon juice	*1 tbsp.*	*15 ml.*	*1 tbsp.*
Soured cream	*¼ pt.*	*150 ml.*	*⅔ cup*
Pinch of salt			
Orange	*1*	*1*	*1*
Apricot jam	*2 tbsp.*	*2 tbsp.*	*2 tbsp.*
Double cream	*¼ pt.*	*150 ml.*	*⅔ cup*

Put the butter into an 8 ins./20 cm. china flan dish and heat in the microwave oven for 1 minute until melted. Crush the biscuits into crumbs and stir into the butter with 1 oz./25 g./2 tablespoons sugar. Press over the sides and base of the flan dish to form a shell. Cream the cheese in a bowl with the remaining sugar and eggs. Make sure that the orange juice has thawed, and work into the mixture with lemon juice, soured cream and salt. Pour into the crumb case. Microwave for 2 minutes. Leave to stand for 2 minutes and then microwave for 2 minutes. Leave to stand for 1 minute and microwave again for 1 minute. Leave until cold. Peel the orange and cut out the segments with a sharp knife. Melt the apricot jam and brush on the surface of the cheesecake. Whip the cream and pipe on to the cheesecake and decorate with orange segments.

Fruit Sponge

✱ 2 months Serves 4

INGREDIENTS	Imperial	Metric	American
Eating apples	*1 lb.*	*450 g.*	*1 lb.*
Canned apricots	*8 oz.*	*225 g.*	*8 oz.*
Margarine	*2 oz.*	*50 g.*	*4 tbsp.*
Caster sugar	*2 oz.*	*50 g.*	*4 tbsp.*
Egg	*1*	*1*	*1*
Self-raising flour	*2 oz.*	*50 g.*	*½ cup*
Chopped walnuts	*2 oz.*	*50 g.*	*½ cup*

Peel and core the apples and cut them into thin slices. Put into a pie dish with the drained apricots and spoon on 3 tablespoons syrup from the can. Cook in the microwave oven for 5 minutes. Cream the margarine and caster sugar until light and fluffy. Work in the egg and fold in the flour and walnuts. Spread over the fruit. Microwave for 6 minutes. Leave to stand for 3 minutes and serve with cream or ice cream.

REHEAT
10 minutes

SPECIAL INSTRUCTIONS
Open-freeze before wrapping. For freezing, add a little sugar to cream when whipping.

THAW
At room temperature 3 hours

Baked Walnut Cheesecake

* 2 months Serves 8

INGREDIENTS	Imperial	Metric	American
Butter or margarine	*2 oz.*	*50 g.*	*4 tbsp.*
Digestive biscuits (Graham crackers)	*12*	*12*	*12*
Caster sugar	*1 oz.*	*25 g.*	*2 tbsp.*
Dark soft brown sugar	*3 oz.*	*75 g.*	*½ cup*
Plain flour	*2 tsp.*	*2 tsp.*	*2 tsp.*
Full fat soft cream cheese	*8 oz.*	*225 g.*	*8 oz.*
Egg	*1*	*1*	*1*
Vanilla essence	*¼ tsp.*	*¼ tsp.*	*¼ tsp.*
Chopped walnuts	*1 oz.*	*25 g.*	*¼ cup*
Maple syrup	*2 tbsp.*	*2 tbsp.*	*2 tbsp.*
Walnut halves	*12*	*12*	*12*

Put the butter into an 8 ins./20 cm. china flan dish and heat in the microwave oven for 1 minute until melted. Crush the biscuits into crumbs and stir into the butter with the sugar. Press over the sides and base of the flan dish to form a shell. Stir together the brown sugar and flour and work in the cream cheese. Beat very well until combined and work in the egg, vanilla essence and chopped walnuts. Put into the crumb case. Cook in the microwave oven for 7 minutes. Chill for 8 hours or overnight. Just before serving, brush top with maple syrup and decorate with walnut halves.

THAW
At room temperature 3 hours

Christmas Pudding

* 2 months Serves 6

INGREDIENTS	Imperial	Metric	American
Sultanas (white raisins)	*8 oz.*	*225 g.*	*1⅓ cups*
Raisins	*8 oz.*	*225 g.*	*1⅓ cups*
Currants	*4 oz.*	*100 g.*	*⅔ cup*
Chopped mixed peel	*2 oz.*	*50 g.*	*⅓ cup*
Carrot	*1 medium*	*1 medium*	*1 medium*
Plain flour	*4 oz.*	*100 g.*	*1 cup*
Fine brown breadcrumbs	*4 oz.*	*100 g.*	*2 cups*
Dark soft brown sugar	*4 oz.*	*100 g.*	*⅔ cup*
Butter, softened	*4 oz.*	*100 g.*	*½ cup*
Black treacle	*2 tbsp.*	*2 tbsp.*	*2 tbsp.*
Eggs	*2*	*2*	*2*
Brandy or milk	*4 tbsp.*	*60 ml.*	*4 tbsp.*
Lemon juice	*1 tbsp.*	*15 ml.*	*1 tbsp.*
Grated lemon rind	*2 tsp.*	*2 tsp.*	*2 tsp.*
Ground mixed spice	*1½ tsp.*	*1½ tsp.*	*1½ tsp.*

Mix together all the dried fruit and peel. Grate the carrot finely and stir in. Add all the remaining ingredients and mix very thoroughly. Cover and leave to stand overnight. Put into a lightly greased 2 pint/1 litre pudding basin and cover with clingfilm. Cook in the microwave oven for 5 minutes. Leave to stand for 5 minutes. Microwave for 1 minute. Turn out and serve hot with brandy butter, cream or custard. To keep the pudding, leave to cool with a new piece of clingfilm on the surface. When cold, wrap in greaseproof paper and foil and keep in an airtight container for up to 2 months.

REHEAT
10 minutes

Peach Topper

∗ 2 months Serves 8

INGREDIENTS	Imperial	Metric	American
Canned sliced peaches	*2 lb.*	*900 g.*	*2 lb.*
Plain flour	*1 oz.*	*25 g.*	*2 tbsp.*
Lemon juice	*1 tbsp.*	*15 ml.*	*1 tbsp.*
Vanilla essence	*¼ tsp.*	*¼ tsp.*	*¼ tsp.*
Almond essence	*¼ tsp.*	*¼ tsp.*	*¼ tsp.*
Ground cinnamon	*1 tsp.*	*1 tsp.*	*1 tsp.*
Pinch of salt			
Butter	*1 oz.*	*25 g.*	*2 tbsp.*
Topping			
Plain flour	*2 oz.*	*50 g.*	*½ cup*
Caster sugar	*4 oz.*	*100 g.*	*½ cup*
Baking powder	*½ tsp.*	*½ tsp.*	*½ tsp.*
Pinch of salt			
Butter, softened	*1 oz.*	*25 g.*	*2 tbsp.*
Egg	*1*	*1*	*1*
Ground cinnamon	*1 tsp.*	*1 tsp.*	*1 tsp.*

Drain the peaches and reserve 4 tablespoons syrup. Mix the peaches with this syrup, flour, lemon juice, essences, cinnamon and salt and place in an 8 ins./20 cm. square dish, spreading evenly to the corners. Cut the butter into small pieces and dot on the surface. Beat all the topping ingredients except the cinnamon until they are smooth. Divide into 9 portions and drop at intervals over the peaches. Sprinkle with cinnamon. Cook in the microwave oven for 14 minutes. Serve warm with cream or ice cream.

REHEAT
10 minutes

Rhubarb Crumble

* 2 months Serves 4

INGREDIENTS	Imperial	Metric	American
Rhubarb	*12 oz.*	*350 g.*	*12 oz.*
Caster sugar	*2 oz.*	*50 g.*	*4 tbsp.*
Water	*2 tbsp.*	*30 ml.*	*2 tbsp.*
Butter	*2 oz.*	*50 g.*	*4 tbsp.*
Plain flour	*4 oz.*	*100 g.*	*1 cup*
Dark soft brown sugar	*2 oz.*	*50 g.*	*4 tbsp.*
Chopped walnuts	*2 oz.*	*50 g.*	*½ cup*
Ground mixed spice	*½ tsp.*	*½ tsp.*	*½ tsp.*

Wash the rhubarb and cut into 1 in./2.5 cm. lengths. Put into a pie dish and sprinkle with sugar, and water. Cook in the microwave oven for 5 minutes, stirring twice. Rub the butter into the flour and stir in the sugar, walnuts and spice. Sprinkle on top of the fruit and press very lightly with a fork. Microwave for 4 minutes. Leave to stand for 5 minutes before serving with cream or custard. Apples, plums, gooseberries or blackcurrants may be used instead of rhubarb.

REHEAT
10 minutes

Cranberry Sponge

✱ 2 months Serves 6

INGREDIENTS	Imperial	Metric	American
Fresh or frozen cranberries	*8 oz.*	*225 g.*	*1½ cups*
Sugar	*2½ oz.*	*65 g.*	*⅓ cup*
Egg	*1*	*1*	*1*
Caster sugar	*2 oz.*	*50 g.*	*¼ cup*
Dark soft brown sugar	*1½ oz.*	*40 g.*	*¼ cup*
Plain flour	*2 oz.*	*50 g.*	*½ cup*
Butter or margarine, melted	*4 oz.*	*100 g.*	*½ cup*
Chopped walnuts	*1 oz.*	*25 g.*	*¼ cup*

Grease a 9 ins./22.5 cm. china flan dish. Mix the cranberries and sugar and place in the dish. Cover with clingfilm and cook in the microwave oven for 2 minutes. Beat the egg with the caster sugar, brown sugar, flour and melted fat until well blended. Sprinkle the nuts on the cranberries and pour on the batter, smoothing it to the edges. Microwave for 9 minutes. Serve with cream or ice cream.

REHEAT
10 minutes

CAKES AND BAKES

N.B. It is important to remember that cakes will appear uncooked when taken from a microwave oven. They continue to cook during the standing time. Appearances can be improved, if required, by the addition of icing fancy decorations.

For ease of removal from container, line dishes loosely with clingfilm.

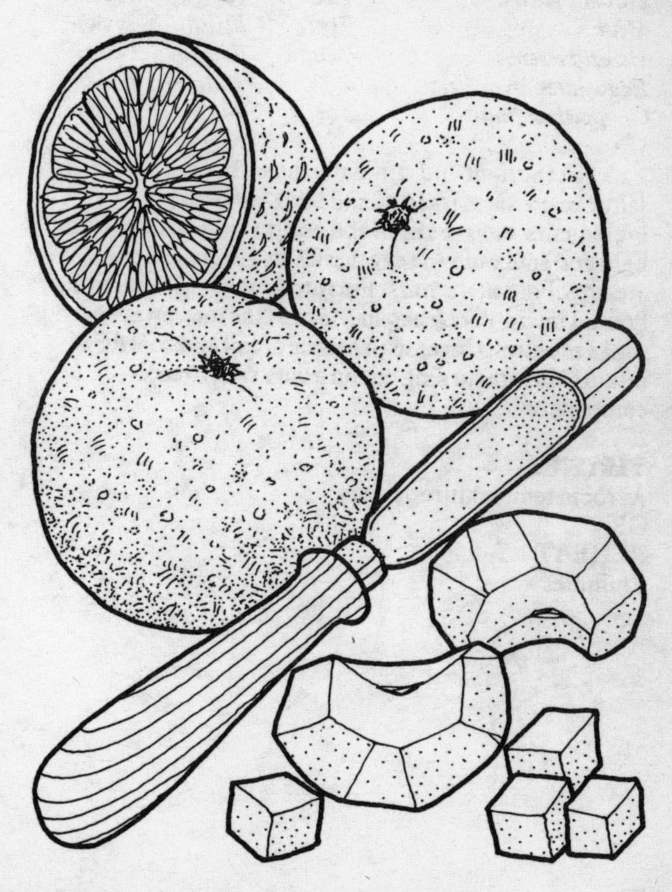

Walnut Loaf

* 2 months

INGREDIENTS	Imperial	Metric	American
Plain flour	*8 oz.*	*225 g.*	*2 cups*
Caster sugar	*10 oz.*	*300 g.*	*1¼ cups*
Baking powder	*1 tsp.*	*1 tsp.*	*1 tsp.*
Salt	*½ tsp.*	*½ tsp.*	*½ tsp.*
Soft margarine	*4 oz.*	*100 g.*	*½ cup*
Milk	*¼ pt.*	*150 ml.*	*⅔ cup*
Vanilla essence	*¼ tsp.*	*¼ tsp.*	*¼ tsp.*
Egg whites	*4*	*4*	*4*
Chopped walnuts	*2 oz.*	*50 g.*	*½ cup*

Sift the flour and stir in the sugar, baking powder and salt. Cream the margarine and work in the dry ingredients. Add the milk and essence and beat hard until light and soft. Add the egg whites and beat hard until creamy. Fold in the nuts. Put into a lightly greased and floured microwave loaf pan. Bake in the microwave oven for 13 minutes. Cover with a piece of foil and cool for 10 minutes before turning out on a wire rack to cool completely.

THAW
At room temperature 3 hours
OR
REHEAT
4 minutes

Nut Cake

✱ 2 months

INGREDIENTS	Imperial	Metric	American
Plain flour	*5 oz.*	*125 g.*	*1¼ cups*
Pinch of salt			
Ground cinnamon	*½ tsp.*	*½ tsp.*	*½ tsp.*
Dark soft brown sugar	*3 oz.*	*75 g.*	*½ cup*
Caster sugar	*3 oz.*	*75 g.*	*⅓ cup*
Vegetable oil	*5 tbsp.*	*75 ml.*	*5 tbsp.*
Chopped walnuts	*1 oz.*	*25 g.*	*¼ cup*
Baking powder	*1 tsp.*	*1 tsp.*	*1 tsp.*
Bicarbonate of soda	*½ tsp.*	*½ tsp.*	*½ tsp.*
Egg	*1*	*1*	*1*
Sour milk	*¼ pt.*	*150 ml.*	*⅔ cup*

Sift the flour, salt and half the cinnamon together. Add the brown and white sugars and the oil and beat until well mixed. Take 6 tablespoons of this mixture and mix with the nuts and the remaining cinnamon. Add the baking powder, soda, egg and milk to the remaining mixture and beat until smooth. Put this mixture into an 8 ins./20 cm. greased round cake dish and sprinkle on the nut mixture. Cook in the microwave oven for 8 minutes. Cool for 10 minutes and serve warm.

REHEAT
4 minutes

Applesauce Cake

* 2 months

INGREDIENTS	Imperial	Metric	American
Plain flour	*6 oz.*	*150 g.*	*1½ cups*
Baking powder	*½ tsp.*	*½ tsp.*	*½ tsp.*
Salt	*½ tsp.*	*½ tsp.*	*½ tsp.*
Ground cloves	*¼ tsp.*	*¼ tsp.*	*¼ tsp.*
Ground nutmeg	*¼ tsp.*	*¼ tsp.*	*¼ tsp.*
Ground allspice	*¼ tsp.*	*¼ tsp.*	*¼ tsp.*
Butter or margarine	*4 oz.*	*100 g.*	*½ cup*
Dark soft brown sugar	*6 oz.*	*150 g.*	*1 cup*
Egg	*1*	*1*	*1*
Unsweetened applesauce	*½ pt.*	*300 ml.*	*1¼ cups*
Seedless raisins	*2 oz.*	*50 g.*	*½ cup*

Lightly grease and flour a shallow square baking dish. Sift together the flour, baking powder, salt and spices. Cream the fat and sugar together until light and fluffy. Work in the egg. Mix the applesauce and raisins together. Add the dry ingredients and the apple mixture alternately to the creamed mixture and beat well. Pour into the baking dish. Bake in the microwave oven for 12 minutes, and cool in the dish before cutting into squares.

For additional eye appeal, sprinkle thickly with icing sugar (for freezing, add after thawing).

SPECIAL INSTRUCTIONS
Freeze in dish and thaw before cutting into squares.

THAW
At room temperature 3 hours

Fudge Cake

✱ 2 months

INGREDIENTS	Imperial	Metric	American
Plain flour	*5 oz.*	*125 g.*	*1¼ cups*
Baking powder	*1 tsp.*	*1 tsp.*	*1 tsp.*
Bicarbonate of soda	*¼ tsp.*	*¼ tsp.*	*¼ tsp.*
Salt	*¼ tsp.*	*¼ tsp.*	*¼ tsp.*
Caster sugar	*10 oz.*	*300 g.*	*1¼ cups*
Soft margarine	*1½ oz.*	*40 g.*	*3 tbsp.*
Milk	*8 fl. oz.*	*200 g.*	*1 cup*
Vanilla essence	*¼ tsp.*	*¼ tsp.*	*¼ tsp.*
Egg	*1*	*1*	*1*
Plain chocolate	*3 oz.*	*75 g.*	*3 squares*
Chopped nuts	*2 oz.*	*50 g.*	*½ cup*
Chocolate butter icing (see page 147)			

Lightly grease and flour two 8 ins./20 cm. round baking dishes. Sift together the flour, baking powder, bicarbonate of soda and salt. Stir in the sugar and then add the margarine, milk and essence. Beat hard until smooth. Add the egg and beat well. Break up the chocolate and put into a bowl. Microwave for 2 minutes. Add to the other ingredients and beat well until smooth and creamy. Stir in the nuts. Divide the mixture between the two baking dishes. Cook each one separately in the microwave oven for 8 minutes. Cool in the dishes with a piece of foil over the top for 10 minutes, and then turn on to a wire rack to cool. Fill and top the cake with chocolate butter icing.

SPECIAL INSTRUCTIONS
Open-freeze before wrapping.

THAW
At room temperature 3 hours

Chocolate Squares

∗ 2 months

INGREDIENTS	Imperial	Metric	American
Butter	*2 oz.*	*50 g.*	*¼ cup*
Sugar	*½ tsp.*	*½ tsp.*	*½ tsp.*
Plain flour	*3 oz.*	*75 g.*	*¾ cup*
Egg yolk	*1*	*1*	*1*
Water	*1 tbsp.*	*15 ml.*	*1 tbsp.*
Plain chocolate	*6 oz.*	*150 g.*	*6 squares*
Topping			
Butter	*1½ oz.*	*40 g.*	*3 tbsp.*
Sugar	*2 oz.*	*50 g.*	*¼ cup*
Egg	*1*	*1*	*1*
Vanilla essence	*½ tsp.*	*½ tsp.*	*½ tsp.*
Chopped walnuts	*4 oz.*	*100 g.*	*1 cup*

Cream the butter and work in the sugar, flour, egg yolk and water. Spread the mixture evenly in an 8 ins./20 cm. square dish. Cook in the microwave oven for 2 minutes. Grate the chocolate or chop it finely. Sprinkle over the baked mixture and heat for 1 minute. Spread the melted chocolate evenly and leave to stand for 10 minutes until the chocolate has almost hardened. Put the butter into a bowl and heat in the microwave oven for 30 seconds. Add the remaining ingredients and spread over the chocolate. Bake for 6 minutes. Cool and cut into squares.

SPECIAL INSTRUCTIONS
Freeze in dish and cut in squares when thawed.

THAW
At room temperature 3 hours

Orange Juice Cake

* 2 months

INGREDIENTS	Imperial	Metric	American
Eggs	*2*	*2*	*2*
Caster sugar	*4 oz.*	*100 g.*	*½ cup*
Plain flour	*9 oz.*	*275 g.*	*2¼ cups*
Granulated sugar	*8 oz.*	*225 g.*	*1 cup*
Baking powder	*3 tsp.*	*3 tsp.*	*3 tsp.*
Salt	*½ tsp.*	*½ tsp.*	*½ tsp.*
Vegetable oil	*4 tbsp.*	*30 ml.*	*4 tbsp.*
Unsweetened orange juice	*8 fl. oz.*	*200 ml.*	*1 cup*
Orange glacé icing and butter icing (see page 147)			

Separate the eggs and whisk the egg whites to soft peaks. Beat in the caster sugar a little at a time until the mixture is stiff and glossy. Put the flour, granulated sugar, baking powder, salt, oil and half the orange juice into a bowl and beat hard until thoroughly mixed. Add the remaining orange juice and egg yolks and beat hard until light and soft. Fold in the egg white mixture. Put the mixture into two lightly greased and floured 8 ins./20 cm. round baking dishes. Bake each one in the microwave oven for 8 minutes. Leave to cool in the dishes, covered with foil. After 5 minutes, turn on to a wire rack and leave until cold. Put the layers together with butter icing and cover top with glacé icing.

SPECIAL INSTRUCTIONS
Freeze without glacé icing. Ice cake after thawing.

THAW
At room temperature 3 hours

Banana Bread

∗ 2 months

INGREDIENTS	Imperial	Metric	American
Plain flour	*7 oz.*	*200 g.*	*1¾ cups*
Baking powder	*1½ tsp.*	*1½ tsp.*	*1½ tsp.*
Bicarbonate of soda	*½ tsp.*	*½ tsp.*	*½ tsp.*
Salt	*½ tsp.*	*½ tsp.*	*½ tsp.*
Ripe bananas	*2*	*2*	*2*
Lemon juice	*1 tbsp.*	*15 ml.*	*1 tbsp.*
Butter or margarine	*3 oz.*	*75 g.*	*6 tbsp.*
Caster sugar	*6 oz.*	*150 g.*	*¾ cup*
Eggs	*2*	*2*	*2*
Milk	*4 tbsp.*	*30 ml.*	*4 tbsp.*
Chopped walnuts	*2 oz.*	*50 g.*	*½ cup*

Lightly grease and flour a microwave loaf pan. Sift together the flour, baking powder, bicarbonate of soda and salt. Mash the bananas and lemon juice in another bowl. Cream the butter or margarine and sugar until light and fluffy and work in the eggs one at a time, beating well after each addition. Add the dry ingredients and milk alternately, and beat well. Fold in the walnuts and the banana mixture. Put into the prepared loaf pan and bake for 13 minutes. Cool in the pan with a piece of foil on top for 10 minutes, then turn on to a wire rack to cool completely.

For additional eye appeal, cover top with lemon glacé icing.

THAW
At room temperature 3 hours
OR
REHEAT
4 minutes

Butter Icing

INGREDIENTS	Imperial	Metric	American
Icing sugar (confectioner's sugar)	*4 oz.*	*100 g.*	*½ cup*
Butter	*2 oz.*	*50 g.*	*4 tbsp.*
Orange	*1 small*	*1 small*	*1 small*

Beat the butter until light and fluffy. Beat in the sugar, and then add the finely grated orange rind, and about 2 teaspoons of the juice.

Glacé Icing

INGREDIENTS	Imperial	Metric	American
Icing sugar (confectioner's sugar)	*2 oz.*	*50 g.*	*¼ cup*
Orange juice	*2–3 tbsp.*	*2–3 tbsp.*	*2–3 tbsp.*

Sieve the icing sugar (confectioner's sugar). Add the orange juice and enough cold water to form a smooth cream.

Chocolate Butter Icing

INGREDIENTS	Imperial	Metric	American
Icing sugar (confectioners sugar)	*6 oz.*	*170 g.*	*¾ cup*
Butter	*3 oz.*	*80 g.*	*6 tbsp.*
Cocoa powder	*1 tbsp.*	*1 tbsp.*	*1 tbsp.*

Cream the cocoa powder with a little cold water to form a paste. Beat the butter until light and fluffy, and add the icing sugar (confectioners sugar). Beat well, then mix in the cocoa paste.

Golden Cake

* 2 months

INGREDIENTS	Imperial	Metric	American
Plain flour	*8 oz.*	*225 g.*	*2 cups*
Baking powder	*2 tsp.*	*2 tsp.*	*2 tsp.*
Salt	*1/4 tsp.*	*1/4 tsp.*	*1/4 tsp.*
Soft margarine	*4 oz.*	*100 g.*	*1/2 cup*
Caster sugar	*4 oz.*	*100 g.*	*1/2 cup*
Vanilla essence	*1/4 tsp.*	*1/4 tsp.*	*1/4 tsp.*
Eggs	*2*	*2*	*2*
Milk	*4 tbsp.*	*60 ml.*	*4 tbsp.*
Icing sugar (confectioner's sugar)	*4 oz.*	*100 g.*	*1/2 cup*
Butter	*2 oz.*	*50 g.*	*4 tbsp.*

Sift together the flour, baking powder and salt. Cream the margarine with the sugar until light and fluffy. Work in the vanilla and eggs. Add the flour mixture alternately with the milk. Grease and flour lightly two 8 ins./20 cm. round baking dishes. Put half the mixture into each dish. Cook each cake separately in the microwave oven for 7 minutes. Cover the top of the cakes with foil as they cool for 5 minutes and then turn on to a rack to become cold. Beat the butter until soft, then mix in the sieved icing (confectioner's) sugar. Fill and top the cake with this mixture. Flavourings and/or colourings (such as almond or vanilla essence) may be added to the butter icing.

SPECIAL INSTRUCTIONS
Open-freeze before wrapping.

THAW
At room temperature 3 hours

Chocolate Almond Cake

* 2 months

INGREDIENTS	Imperial	Metric	American
Butter or margarine	*4 oz.*	*100 g.*	*½ cup*
Caster sugar	*4 oz.*	*100 g.*	*½ cup*
Eggs	*2*	*2*	*2*
Self-raising flour	*4 oz.*	*100 g.*	*1 cup*
Cocoa powder	*2 oz.*	*50 g.*	*4 tbsp.*
Ground almonds	*2 oz.*	*50 g.*	*½ cup*
Milk	*¼ pt.*	*150 ml.*	*⅔ cup*
Golden syrup (corn syrup)	*4 tbsp.*	*4 tbsp.*	*4 tbsp.*
Blanched almonds	*8–9*	*8–9*	*8–9*
Icing			
Plain chocolate	*4 oz.*	*100 g.*	*4 squares*
Butter	*1 oz.*	*25 g.*	*2 tbsp.*

Cream the butter or margarine and the sugar until light and fluffy. Beat in the eggs one at a time. Sift the flour and cocoa powder together and fold into the mixture. Fold in the ground almonds. Add the milk and syrup and beat well until light and soft. Put into an 8 ins./20 cm. cake dish lined with clingfilm. Cook in the microwave oven for 4 minutes. Take out of the oven and cover the top with foil while the cake cools. Turn out on a wire rack and leave until completely cold. Break up the chocolate and put into a bowl with the butter. Microwave for 2 minutes. Beat well. Dip the blanched almonds in the icing so they are half coated, and leave to dry on a cooling rack. Pour the rest of the icing over the cake so that it runs down the sides as well. Decorate with the chocolate covered almonds.

SPECIAL INSTRUCTIONS
Open-freeze before wrapping.

THAW
At room temperature 3 hours

Spiced Bran Cakes

* 2 months

INGREDIENTS	Imperial	Metric	American
Plain flour	*6 oz.*	*150 g.*	*1½ cups*
Baking powder	*2 tsp.*	*2 tsp.*	*2 tsp.*
Ground mixed spice	*2 tsp.*	*2 tsp.*	*2 tsp.*
Salt	*½ tsp.*	*½ tsp.*	*½ tsp.*
All Bran cereal	*3 oz.*	*75 g.*	*1½ cups*
Milk	*8 fl. oz.*	*200 ml.*	*1 cup*
Sugar	*2½ oz.*	*65 g.*	*⅓ cup*
Vegetable oil	*3 tbsp.*	*45 ml.*	*3 tbsp.*
Egg	*1*	*1*	*1*
Seedless raisins	*3 oz.*	*75 g.*	*¾ cup*
Grated orange rind	*1 tbsp.*	*1 tbsp.*	*1 tbsp.*

Sift together the flour, baking powder, spice and salt. Put the bran into the milk and leave to stand for 10 minutes. Beat into the flour with the remaining ingredients. Divide the mixture between 15 cake cases. Put each into a microwave cake tray (this will take 5 cakes). If a special tray is not available, put each cake into a custard cup or coffee cup. Cook in the microwave oven for 4 minutes. Repeat for remaining cakes.

For additional eye appeal, cover tops with lemon or orange glacé icing.

THAW
At room temperature 1 hour

Crumb Cake

* 2 months

INGREDIENTS	Imperial	Metric	American
Caster sugar	*10 oz.*	*300 g.*	*1¼ cups*
Plain flour	*8 oz.*	*225 g.*	*2 cups*
Baking powder	*2 tsp.*	*2 tsp.*	*2 tsp.*
Ground cinnamon	*1 tsp.*	*1 tsp.*	*1 tsp.*
Butter or margarine	*4 oz.*	*100 g.*	*½ cup*
Eggs	*2*	*2*	*2*
Milk	*7 tbsp.*	*100 ml.*	*7 tbsp.*

Stir together the sugar, flour, baking powder and cinnamon. Soften the butter and margarine and work into the dry ingredients until thoroughly mixed. Set aside one-quarter of the mixture. Mix the eggs and milk with the remaining mixture and beat well. Put into a lightly greased and floured 8 ins./20 cm. square baking dish. Sprinkle the remaining mixture on top in an even layer. Bake in the microwave oven for 10 minutes. Cool completely in the dish before cutting into squares.

SPECIAL INSTRUCTIONS
Freeze in dish, and cut in squares after thawing.

THAW
At room temperature 3 hours

Chocolate Brownies

* 2 months

INGREDIENTS	Imperial	Metric	American
Plain chocolate	*2 oz.*	*50 g.*	*2 squares*
Butter or margarine	*3 oz.*	*75 g.*	*6 tbsp.*
Dark soft brown sugar	*6 oz.*	*150 g.*	*1 cup*
Eggs	*2*	*2*	*2*
Plain flour	*5 oz.*	*125 g.*	*1¼ cups*
Baking powder	*¼ tsp.*	*¼ tsp.*	*¼ tsp.*
Vanilla essence	*½ tsp.*	*½ tsp.*	*½ tsp.*
Milk	*2 tbsp.*	*30 ml.*	*2 tbsp.*
Icing sugar (confectioners sugar)	*2 oz.*	*50 g.*	*¼ cup*

Break up the chocolate and put it into a bowl with the butter or margarine. Heat in the microwave oven for 2 minutes. Beat in the sugar and eggs until smooth. Sift the flour with the baking powder. Add to the chocolate mixture with the essence and milk and beat until smooth. Put into a greased rectangular baking dish. Cook in the microwave oven for 7 minutes. Cool in the dish for 10 minutes, and dust the top thickly with sieved icing (confectioners) sugar. Cut into squares and lift on to a rack to cool. If preferred, cover the surface of the cake with 4 oz./100 g./4 squares of melted plain chocolate instead of sugar.

SPECIAL INSTRUCTIONS
Cover with icing sugar or melted plain chocolate when thawed.

THAW
At room temperature 3 hours

Apple Cake

* 2 months

INGREDIENTS	Imperial	Metric	American
Butter or margarine	*6 oz.*	*150 g.*	*¾ cup*
Caster sugar	*4 oz.*	*100 g.*	*½ cup*
Eggs	*3*	*3*	*3*
Golden syrup (corn syrup)	*2 tbsp.*	*2 tbsp.*	*2 tbsp.*
Lemon	*1*	*1*	*1*
Self-raising flour	*6 oz.*	*150 g.*	*1½ cups*
Chopped walnuts	*2 oz.*	*50 g.*	*½ cup*
Eating apple	*1*	*1*	*1*
Icing sugar (confectioner's sugar)	*4 oz.*	*100 g.*	*½ cup*
Lemon juice	*2 tbsp.*	*30 ml.*	*2 tbsp.*
Walnut halves	*9*	*9*	*9*

Cream the butter or margarine and sugar until light and fluffy. Add the beaten eggs and then the golden (corn) syrup. Grate the lemon rind and squeeze out the juice. Work into the mixture and then fold in the flour and chopped nuts. Peel and core the apple, and cut into small dice. Fold into the cake mixture. Put into an 8 ins./20 cm. cake dish and bake in the microwave oven for 4 minutes. Remove from the oven and leave to stand with a piece of foil over the top. When cool, turn out on a rack and leave until cold. Mix the sieved icing sugar with the lemon juice and enough water to form a smooth paste. Cover the top of the cake with lemon icing and decorate with walnut halves.

SPECIAL INSTRUCTIONS
Freeze without glacé icing. Ice and decorate with walnuts when thawed.

THAW
At room temperature 3 hours

Jam Crumble Squares

* 2 months

INGREDIENTS	Imperial	Metric	American
Butter or margarine	*6 oz.*	*150 g.*	*¾ cup*
Dark soft brown sugar	*6 oz.*	*150 g.*	*1 cup*
Plain flour	*7 oz.*	*200 g.*	*1¾ cups*
Salt	*½ tsp.*	*½ tsp.*	*½ tsp.*
Baking powder	*½ tsp.*	*½ tsp.*	*½ tsp.*
Porridge oats	*6 oz.*	*150 g.*	*1½ cups*
Raspberry jam	*4 oz.*	*100 g.*	*¾ cup*

Lightly grease an 8 ins./20 cm. square baking dish. Cream the fat and sugar together until light and fluffy. Stir in the flour, salt, baking powder and oats and mix thoroughly. Press half the mixture into the baking dish. Melt the jam in the microwave for 30 seconds and spread evenly over this base. Crumble on the remaining oat mixture, pressing down lightly. Bake in the microwave oven for 7 minutes. Cut into squares and cool in the baking dish.

SPECIAL INSTRUCTIONS
Freeze in dish, and cut in squares after thawing.

THAW
At room temperature 3 hours

Fruitcake Squares

∗ 2 months

INGREDIENTS	Imperial	Metric	American
Butter or margarine	*1½ oz.*	*40 g.*	*3 tbsp.*
Digestive biscuits (Graham crackers)	9	9	9
Desiccated coconut	*2 oz.*	*50 g.*	*½ cup*
Chopped mixed peel	*4 oz.*	*100 g.*	*1 cup*
Dates	*2 oz.*	*50 g.*	*½ cup*
Plain flour	*½ oz.*	*15 g.*	*1 tbsp.*
Chopped walnuts	*4 oz.*	*100 g.*	*1 cup*
Sweetened condensed milk	*¼ pt.*	*150 ml.*	*⅔ cup*
Glacé cherries, chopped	*1 oz.*	*25 g.*	*¼ cup*

Put the butter or margarine into an 8 ins./20 cm. square baking dish and heat in the microwave oven for 30 seconds until melted. Crush the biscuits into crumbs. Stir into the butter and spread the mixture evenly over the base of the baking dish. Sprinkle with coconut, and then sprinkle the peel on top. Chop the dates finely and mix with the flour. Sprinkle the date mixture on top of the peel and then sprinkle with nuts. Pour the milk evenly over the top. Cook in the microwave oven for 8 minutes. Cool in the baking dish and cut into squares to serve.

SPECIAL INSTRUCTIONS
Freeze in dish, and cut in squares after thawing.

THAW
At room temperature 3 hours

Chocolate Date Bars

* 2 months

INGREDIENTS	Imperial	Metric	American
Dates	*2 oz.*	*50 g.*	*½ cup*
Boiling water	*4 tbsp.*	*60 ml.*	*4 tbsp.*
Caster sugar	*6 oz.*	*150 g.*	*1 cup*
Butter or margarine	*2½ oz.*	*65 g.*	*⅓ cup*
Egg	*1*	*1*	*1*
Plain flour	*4 oz.*	*100 g.*	*1 cup*
Baking powder	*½ tsp.*	*½ tsp.*	*½ tsp.*
Salt	*¼ tsp.*	*¼ tsp.*	*¼ tsp.*
Cocoa powder	*2 tsp.*	*2 tsp.*	*2 tsp.*
Caster sugar	*2 oz.*	*50 g.*	*¼ cup*
Chopped nuts	*1 oz.*	*25 g.*	*¼ cup*
Plain chocolate	*4 oz.*	*100 g.*	*4 squares*

Chop the dates and pour on the water. Leave to stand until cool. Lightly grease and flour an 8 ins./20 cm. square baking dish. Cream 4 oz./100 g./½ cup of the sugar with the butter or margarine until light and fluffy. Work in the egg. Sift together the flour, baking powder, salt and cocoa powder. Add date and flour mixtures alternately to the creamed mixture. Spread in the prepared dish and smooth the top. Mix the remaining caster sugar, nuts and finely chopped chocolate. Sprinkle over the cake mixture and press lightly. Cook in the microwave oven for 8 minutes. Leave to cool in the dish before cutting into squares.

SPECIAL INSTRUCTIONS

Freeze in dish and cut in squares when thawed.

THAW

At room temperature 3 hours

Quick Cheese Bread

✱ 2 months

INGREDIENTS	Imperial	Metric	American
Plain flour	*8 oz.*	*225 g.*	*2 cups*
Baking powder	*2 tsp.*	*2 tsp.*	*2 tsp.*
Mustard powder	*2 tsp.*	*2 tsp.*	*2 tsp.*
Salt	*½ tsp.*	*½ tsp.*	*½ tsp.*
Grated Cheddar cheese	*5 oz.*	*125 g.*	*1¼ cups*
Butter or margarine	*2 oz.*	*50 g.*	*¼ cup*
Milk	*8 fl. oz.*	*200 ml.*	*1 cup*
Eggs	*2*	*2*	*2*

Stir together the flour, baking powder, mustard, salt in a bowl. Add 4 oz./100 g./1 cup cheese. Put the butter into a small bowl and heat in the microwave oven for 1 minute. Stir in the milk and eggs and mix lightly until just blended. Add to the flour and beat until well mixed. Put into a microwave loaf dish and cook in the microwave oven for 9 minutes. Sprinkle the top with remaining cheese and cover with foil so that it does not touch the top. Leave to stand for 20 minutes and turn out. Serve with salad.

THAW
At room temperature 3 hours
OR
REHEAT
4 minutes

INDEX

Apple and Apricote Compôte 127
Apple Betty 126
Apple Cake 153
Apple Sauce 120
Apples, Baked 125
Applesauce Cake 142
Aubergine Casserole 102

Banana Bread 146
Barbecue Sauce 119
Beans and Corn, Creamed 103
Beef, Burgundy 66
Beef Curry 68
Beef Olives 67
Borsch 34
Bran Cakes, Spiced 150
Bread Sauce 115
Butterscotch Sauce 122

Cabbage Casserole, Red 109
Cabbage in Tomato Sauce, Stuffed 110
cakes and bakes 139-157
Cannelloni 97
Carrot Soup 35
Carrots, Orange Glazed 104
Cauliflower Cheese 102
Cheese Bread, Quick ... 157
Cheese Sauce 114
Cheesecake, Baked Orange 132
Cheesecake, Baked Walnut 134
Chicken, Barbecued 93
Chicken, Chinese 90
Chicken, Creamed 88
Chicken Curry 85
Chicken Drumsticks, Herbed 87
Chicken, Herbed Lemon 84
Chicken, Indian 86
Chicken, Italian 83
Chicken Liver Pâté 44
Chicken Livers, Herbed 94
Chicken, Orange 91
Chilli con Carne 80
Chocolate Almond Cake 149
Chocolate Brownies 152
Chocolate Date Bars ... 156
Chocolate Sauce 121
Chocolate Squares 144
Chocolate Walnut Upside-Down Pudding 131
Christmas Pudding 135
Cod in Cider Sauce 52
Code in Grapefruit Sauce 53
Cod, Southern 51
convenience foods, cooking 24
Country Pâté 47
Courgettes in Tomato Sauce 108
Crab, Baked 61
Cranberry Sponge 138
Crumb Cake 151
Cumberland Sauce 118
Curry Sauce 116
Custard Sauce 120

defrosting 25-30

Egg Sauce 114
equipment 12-14

fish and shellfish 50-63
fish, cooking times 18
fresh food, cooking
times 15-17
frozen food, reheating ... 31
fruit, cooking times 20
Fruit Sponge 133
Fruitcake Squares 155
Fudge Cake 143

Gammon, Apple 77
Garden Soup 36
Golden Cake 148
Goulash 69
Grapefruit, Golden 46
Green Peas, French 105

Haddock Pâté, Smoked 48
Ham and Cheese Loaf 81

Icing, Butter 147
Icing, Chocolate
Butter 147
Icing, Glacé 147

Jam Crumble Squares 154

Kedgeree 55
Kidneys in Red Wine 79
Kipper Pâté 45

Lamb and Aubergine
Casserole 72
Lamb Chops, Gingered ... 71
leftovers 32
Lemon Butter 121
Lentil Soup 38
Liver, Herbed 78

Macaroni Cheese 99
Mackerel or Herring,
Baked 54
Mackerel Pots 49
meat 64-81
meat, cooking times 17
meat, defrosting 28-30
Meat Balls in Tomato
Sauce 70
Meat Loaf 73
microwave ovens 9
microwave ovens,
controls 9
microwave ovens,
power control 9-10
microwave ovens, types 9
Mushroom Sauce 114
Mushrooms, Stuffed 106

Nut Cake 141

Onion Sauce 114
Onion Soup 40
Orange Juice Cake 145
Oranges, Caramel 130

Parsley Sauce 114
pasta 96-99
pasta, cooking times 19
Pea Soup, Green 37
Peach Topper 136
Pears, Spiced 129
Pitta Pockets 65
Plaice in Wine Sauce,
Stuffed 58
Pork in Cider Sauce 74
Pork, Oriental 75
Potatoes, Stuffed
Baked 112
poultry 82-95
poultry, cooking times ... 18
poultry, defrosting 28-30
Prawns, Creole 60
preparation of food 10

puddings 124-138

quicktips 32

Ratatouille 107
Rhubarb Crumble 137
rice 100
rice, cooking times 19
Rice, Spanish 100

Salmon Loaf 62
Salmon, Poached 56
sauces 113-123
Sausage and Apple
Bake 76
Seafood Curry 63
soups 33-43
Spaghetti Bolognese 98
Spanish Summer Soup 41
Spinach Salad, Hot 104
Spinach Soup 42
starters 44-49
Strawberry Shortcake 128
Sweet and Sour Sauce 123

timing 11
timing conversion
table 11
Tomato Sauce 117
Tomato Soup 43
Tomatoes, Stuffed 111
Trout in Wine Sauce 57
Trout with Almonds 59
Turkey Bake 92
Turkey, Sweet and
Sour 95

using a microwave 8

Vegetable Soup, Italian 39
vegetables 101-112
vegetables, blanching 22
vegetables, cooking
frozen 23
vegetables, cooking
times 15-16

Walnut Loaf 140
White Sauce 114